PRAISE FOR WASTED

'Intricately crafted...An intimate portrait of a grieving family and a nation unable to reconcile itself to the harmful effects of its drinking culture...Reminiscent of writers such as Chloe Hooper and Helen Garner.' BOOKS+PUBLISHING

'A stunning evocation of grief...Out of the ruins of a young man's life, Muir has created a fundamental challenge to Australians: let's talk about booze.' GUARDIAN

'So achingly beautiful and assured, Helen Garner might be pleased to hand her the keys to the creative nonfiction kingdom and ride off into the Carlton sunset.' SATURDAY PAPER

'[Elspeth Muir] writes beautifully and honestly.' MAMAMIA

'The strongest new Australian voice I've come across this year.' READINGS BLOG

'[Muir] concludes of her brother's death, "What a waste of a life that was." Yet by determinedly documenting the drinking culture that coddled him, she has opened vital new lines of enquiry into our duty of care towards drinkers. It's a tragedy, but now, not entirely a waste.' LIFTED BROW

'Timely and eye-opening...Interweaving brilliant reportage with memoir, *Wasted* delves into Australia's complicated relationship with alcohol.' CANBERRA WEEKLY

'Muir's depiction of Brisbane's tropical climate, its animals and bugs, feels both wholly original and incredibly accurate, and as [the book] continues what emerges is something incredibly upsetting and moving.' CHRIS SOMERVILLE

'[*Wasted*] is a book that had to be written. It is full of compassion and a shining intelligence. It is heartbreaking and funny and full of breathtaking insight.' KRISTINA OLSSON

Elspeth Muir is a Brisbane author whose writing has appeared in the *Lifted Brow*, *The Best of the Lifted Brow: Volume One*, *Griffith Review*, *Voiceworks* and *Bumf*. She is a postgraduate student at the University of Queensland.

Wasted

A story of alcohol, grief and a death in Brisbane

Elspeth Muir

TEXT PUBLISHING MELBOURNE AUSTRALIA

textpublishing.com.au

The Text Publishing Company
Swann House
22 William Street
Melbourne Victoria 3000
Australia

This book started life as an essay, 'Pissed Off', in *Griffith Review 36: What Is Australia For?* (2012)

First published in 2016 by The Text Publishing Company
Reprinted 2016

Cover art by W. H. Chong
Book design by Jessica Horrocks
Typeset in Joanna MT by J & M Typesetting

Printed in Australia by Griffin Press, an Accredited ISO AS/NZS 14001:2004 Environmental Management System printer.

National Library of Australia Cataloguing-in-Publication entry
ISBN: 9781922182135 (paperback)
ISBN: 9781925095135 (ebook)
Creator: Muir, Elspeth, author.
Title: Wasted : a story of alcohol, grief and a death in Brisbane / by Elspeth Muir.
Subjects: Muir, Elspeth—Family. Brothers and sisters—Queensland—Biography.
Young adults—Alcohol use—Australia. Alcoholism—Australia.
Dewey Number: 362.292092

This book is printed on paper certified against the Forest Stewardship Council® Standards. Griffin Press holds FSC chain-of-custody certification SGS-COC-005088. FSC promotes environmentally responsible, socially beneficial and economically viable management of the world's forests.

For Dymphna, Chris, Patrick
and Alexander Muir

CONTENTS

1

THE RIVER

It was hot when Alexander was buried, on one of those low Brisbane mornings in November when you might have scooped a fistful of blue from the sky if you'd stretched an arm out. Hot smells—jasmine, scrub, beer, dirt, exhaust fumes, cigarettes, stinkbugs, grass and rotting mangoes—crystallised in the heavy tropical air that turns southerners mad with despair: *The temperature's not as high as back home, but the goddamned humidity!* Crickets fucked in the bougainvillea and their creaking hum was the hum of the heat—like the muffled roar of a far-off highway, only noticeable when it ceased.

There were flies in the kitchen, cane toads on the driveway, golden-orb spiders in the camellia and mosquitoes in the window blinds. Currawongs, butcherbirds and magpies sang and shat in the frangipani tree while lizards hunted on the pool tiles. At night possums crawled along the brush fence, and bats fought over greenish bananas. Everything, but my brother, was alive.

The funeral was held in a redbrick church on a hill. From the front steps you could see Mount Cootha, St Lucia, The Grange, Hamilton, Ashgrove, Alderley and the city. Light muddied by dust motes spotlit sections of the wooden pews. A crucifix hung high in the curved recess behind the altar, and in the choir loft organ pipes rose like bamboo.

In the aisle the casket rested on a silver trolley with collapsible legs. Frangipani boughs from the tree outside my parents' kitchen were wired into a messy funeral wreath. Beneath the lid was my brother's soggy body—fresh from the refrigerator—pickled in embalming fluids, alcohol and river water. On once-fertile plains of flesh, now flushed with chemicals and emptied of organs, dying parasites weakly tapped their tails. Later, corpse eaters would digest his freckled skin and rough hands. At this moment, however, the microscopic ecosystems had been halted long enough that the stench of their unsavoury feast did not haul the congregation back to earth, dirt, the mechanical minutiae of change—atoms once clumped desegregating and reforming.

It was 2009, and Alexander had just turned twenty-one.

The church was stuffed with people, too many to sit inside, so they stood around the back door peering in. Now and then someone would clutch at my shoulders, or pass me tissues and water. I looked at my hands. Eye contact elicited tearful stares, the endless professions of sympathy: 'I'm sorry for your loss,' 'I'm sorry for your loss,' 'I'm sorry for your loss.' (Fuck off.)

Three priests, dressed in white cotton soutanes, said Mass. Twice, while the others sat, fluffing and smoothing their vestments around them like bantam wings, the tallest priest stood up—unfathomably, incorrectly—as if powered by a broken spring: during the First Reading, then during the Gospel Acclamation. The head priest, irritated, flicked his eyes to glare up at him, but the tall priest clasped his hands at the waist, thrust his medieval beard defiantly towards the sidewall and maintained his steady gaze out the window. It was the type of absurd behaviour my brother loved. For a second I forgot he wasn't there and turned to point it out to him.

I expected that any minute the enormity of his death would collapse an internal wall and feelings would flood my body. Instead, I remained impermeable, almost completely devoid of sensation except, curiously, for my saliva, which tasted bitter.

It was a nice feeling in some ways, like floating in yolk.

The Mass went for an hour. When it finished we followed the casket down the aisle and out the front door, and watched it being loaded into the back of the hearse. My parents and other brother were sucked into the throng of people, and I was by myself. It was hard to know what to say, and no one seemed to know what to say to me, so I stood pleating my dress in one sweaty fist.

Alexander's godfather stood at the church gate, about twenty metres down the hill. As the hearse rolled down the driveway he squeezed a set of bagpipes under his arm and began to play. He was flushed from the heat and his face matched the red on his kilt.

I didn't know he could play the bagpipes. It was charming, both funny and sad.

We followed the hearse to a grass cemetery on the outskirts of Brisbane. There was no shade, so a cemetery employee had erected a cheap marquee over the hole. It was the type of marquee used to shade sausage sizzles at hardware stores; its flimsy legs and shiny plastic cloth were strangely festive.

A mound of dirt was piled high beside the red gash in the ground. Already some enterprising ants were colonising it. I watched as they walked in single file to the top and entered a tunnel.

My brother's coffin rested on batons over the ditch. An undertaker had unscrewed the faux-metal-and-fibreboard crucifix from the lid so we could keep it as a memento. Mum gave it to me a few days later. Jesus' face was clumpy and there was a line down the centre where his body, made up of two separate plastic segments, joined together.

When Alexander was alive I liked to slide my fingers through his messy curls until they snagged. I wanted to do it one last time, but at the funeral parlour, a few nights beforehand, we had been advised not to look at his corpse. Afterwards, in the yellow light outside my grandma's back door, I cried about this, briefly. An aunt, who was going inside, stopped. 'Oh, Els,' she said. 'It's better. He'd been in the river too long.' I nodded, not wanting to seem macabre, but it is something that even now I think about.

In life I had known his face better than my own: broken front teeth patched with discoloured dentist's cement, spiky red neck hair, lopsided smile, faded freckles and blue eyes set in loose skin.

It was a good face: laughing, naughty and intelligent. It caused the people who looked at it to grin involuntarily. Only the men and women who handled my brother's corpse would know its current state, and this was, in some ways, the face I most wanted to behold: proof of his final, strange and lonely journey, twisting through dark water, above the riverbed.

Alexander was the youngest in our family. For the first part of my life he had been a small, quiet shade. Until he reached high school he would stuff one scratchy hand into mine, the thumb of the other hand into his mouth, and I would reluctantly drag him behind me across roads, through department stores, or to the grocery store. Later, he followed my middle brother, Patrick, who protested his presence with his mouth and with his fists, until they found an uneasy equilibrium, partly because of Alexander's doggedness, and mostly because he grew taller and broader than us both.

In the last few years of his life he stopped needing us. I had become used to him and I felt his loss keenly. I was jealous of his wide circle of friends, I resented his independence and I was in awe of his social grace.

I lived in Melbourne then and, when I came home to visit, occasionally we would go out. He tolerated my company, but didn't seek it. The nights ended with me standing against a wall, drinking quickly and smiling awkwardly, while he threw his limbs and sometimes clothes about in the middle of a dance floor, among old and new admirers. Still, even if he no longer had to slip his hand into mine to go places, at least I was familiar with those places.

Alexander's final journey neatly, completely, snapped the sinews that bound him to us. I wanted to see the way his features had settled because I was curious about the person who came out of the river. I wasn't sure who he was.

That he died in water didn't surprise me. Alexander swam in the ocean in winter and when it was raining and in the deep afternoon when the sharks feed. He swam on open beaches and on days when the wind beat rips into the waves. He swam until his skin and eyes were pink, and his hair stiff with salt, long after his companions had retired with pruney fingers and blue nails.

When he was two he paddled into the middle of our backyard pool. Patrick and I were meant to be watching him but we were fighting over a plastic blow-up boat that had no sides anymore.

'Look,' Patrick said. I thought he would rip the broken boat from my hands, so I didn't move. 'Look,' he said again. 'Look at Alexander. He's in the water.'

I turned around. Alexander was floating three or four metres from the step, his hair a soft circle on the surface of the water. His body hung beneath him and he bobbed up and down softly like a jellyfish.

I heard Mum screaming and let go of the boat. There were only a few metres between us but the water felt as viscous as petroleum jelly. When I touched his skin I grabbed him under the arms and lifted his head above the surface. He gasped and cried and scratched my back, and I carried him with difficulty over to the side of the pool, where Mum snatched him out of my arms. 'You were meant to be watching him!' she yelled.

'We didn't know he would do that!' Patrick and I yelled back.

We were both crying now, too.

'I'm sorry,' she said, calming down. 'I was frightened. Thank you, thank you.' And she wrapped him in a towel and took him inside.

Patrick and I followed her in. We sat on the good leather couch in the living room and no one cared that we were wet. Mum hugged Alexander so hard the water seeped through his towel into her clothes. After a while he stopped crying and stuck his thumb in his mouth.

Patrick said, 'Why did you do that, pally? You know you can't swim.' But Alexander never did say.

One year and two weeks before the day of his funeral, I called him three times. It was his twentieth birthday. The first two times he didn't answer. When he picked up the third time his voice was slow and confused.

'Happy birthday,' I said.

'Thanks, El.'

'Are you having a good day?'

'Can I call you back?'

An hour later he phoned. I asked why he hadn't answered my calls. He told me it was because, when I rang, he was passed out on the riverbank beneath mangroves and a wooden walkway that wound between them. He had woken up, he said, because he had a dream he heard an alarm clock—it was his phone ringing. He pulled his way through layers of murky sleep to find the river sucking at his feet.

I thought this was hilarious. 'You idiot,' I said. 'What happened last night?'

'I honestly don't remember, but I am so hungover,' Alexander said, and I laughed for a long time.

'Where are you now?'

'I walked down to the Story Bridge Hotel, told the bartender it was my birthday, and he gave me a free beer.'

'Oh, Alexander,' I said, in a way, I imagine, that was lip-service scolding but mostly admiring.

When I am maudlin, I imagine the long, dirty, licking river, which coils like a snake on hot sand through the fatty suburbs along its waterline, tasted my brother that morning, but was thwarted before it could suck him right in. It waited a year, watching, flicking its sunlit scales, laying open the promise of soft depths on dark evenings; then, early one morning, his curiosity drove him close again, and it ate him.

When I am not maudlin, I know he was not the victim of an animistic river, and that his death, by drowning, was not foreshadowed by his love of water except that it explains why he was near a river, alone, with a blood-alcohol content of almost 0.25. My brother died because he was drunk, and because the drink made him stupid.

The priest said a few words, and the coffin was mechanically lowered into the hole. When it reached the bottom the mourners took turns throwing scoops of dirt onto it from a silver trowel. We sprinkled the dirt with holy water, flinging the drops from the end of a silver pestle.

No one talked. I could hear flies, skin peeling off skin, saliva-sealed lips opening, muted sobs, sniffles, whispering, good shoes crunching on dry soil. After each person had thrown their shovelful of dirt onto the casket we turned around, walked back to our cars, and drove away.

It was easy to dispose of his body, but when Alexander died the parts of our knowledge pertaining to him, the parts of us that were also Alexander's—the memories, the humour, the mannerisms—were ring-barked. And slowly, they began to wither, so that now I have to take a spoon to my mind and scrape away at my recollections to uncover what lives. No matter how quick, how unexpected, the death of a person is slow.

The wake was held at Alexander's high school in a building overlooking rugby fields and the bush. Small schoolboys in school uniform and knee-high socks carried trays of finger food. Behind a makeshift bar waitstaff in white shirts poured wine and served beer. Young men in black suits and sunglasses stood in uncomfortable circles on the patio, like the monoliths at Stonehenge, swigging XXXX and VB.

We watched a glary montage of family photos projected onto a big screen. Outside, a friend showed me her new tattoo and my aunt smoked cigarettes with one of the priests. The people with me made careful, foamy conversation about nothing in particular.

On my way to the bathroom I was stopped by the husband of one of my mum's friends. He told me his brother had died when he was my age. 'My mum never stops talking about him,' he said. 'You'll have to be prepared for that.'

I was tipsy when we left the school in the early evening. The family and a motley bunch of friends converged on my parents' house for dinner. I sat on the verandah with my aunts and uncles and cousins. We ate, and drank, and told stories. When we had nothing left, my mum's younger sister began singing from *The Sound of Music* and everyone else at the table joined in. We sang 'Edelweiss', 'Lonely Goat' and 'How Do You Solve a Problem Like Maria?' like they were football chants and we were winning. Then one of my aunts jumped in the pool in her clothes, then another, then another. And they looked so silly, my funny, soaking aunts, that I laughed, even though I wasn't sure if this was okay. And, although there were shaking heads and disapproving looks, my mum laughed, too, which was most important.

Later, two of my aunts fought, and everyone left crying and drunk. We didn't know how to act. Our family events were always a wild rumpus. It was hard to figure out a new way of being together.

Maybe it was fitting to get drunk at Alexander's wake. 'He would have wanted it,' people said. And they were probably right, because he was only twenty-one. We drank with a sad urgency, turning the reason for our grief into its elixir.

Around 12 p.m. the next day Mum stood on the back verandah and said, 'I really wish everyone would stop drinking now.'

'Why don't you just ask them to stop?' I said. 'I will.'

She shook her head. 'Just leave them, El. It's been a big day.' And I was glad because I didn't really want to ask them either.

That spring was the last dry one in Brisbane for two years. The following November the clouds set in and the skies opened up.

For three months it rained. It rained so hard my clothes and furniture grew dusty white mould, two pairs of sodden shoes fell apart, the house stank of rot, and unless you had a dryer—which I didn't—washing was always half damp.

By January the river was boiling. I caught the ferry to work until, instead of walking down the jetty to the floating platform, which was usually a few metres beneath the bank, I walked up the jetty. The thickening river swept up logs, loose pylons and shopping trolleys; the debris formed crude coracles that came too close, too quick; and so the service was cancelled.

On the first day of sun for months, the river broke its banks. Waterfront suburbs were flooded with a fetid broth. The river backed up through stormwater drains; formed inland lakes; deposited bull sharks in puddles; sucked up toys, refrigerators, cars and houses; and shut down towns and cities along its reach. Days after the water receded, pockets of air still stunk of sulphur and mildew.

In the muddy aftermath, when the supermarkets were not yet restocked, television helicopters stalked the skies and the people who lived on high land donned gumboots to help out the people who lived on low land, shock at the river's appetite hummed through conversations. Finally, what I felt inside was aligned with the outside world.

I read once that in Russia, to break the drought, peasants would take the corpse of a man who died of drink and bury it in a peat bog. In the months following the flood I found strange and fleeting comfort in wondering if my brother's corpse had brought the rain.

But I doubt it. There are no peat bogs in Brisbane, and I don't think the Pinnaroo Lawn Cemetery looks kindly on do-it-yourself exhumation.

Besides, there was no magic in Alexander's death. It was a waste.

2

LO SIENTO

My brother died in an accident. At least, everyone who knew him was fairly sure it was an accident, but it might also have been design. He had a history of doing stupid things when he was drunk and, unfortunately, his blood-alcohol level was not quite high enough before he died to cause him to pass out. The police were able to identify his body from his fingerprints. They were on file from a drunk-and-disorderly arrest.

As the years pass it becomes more difficult to remember him. What he sounded like, his smells, what he wore, what he said, his facial expressions. So, when I try to figure out what happened, I start at the beginning, because the memories are less fuzzy there.

Alexander had a convex stomach, and his cloth diapers,

held together with long metal safety pins (which tasted tart and trapped your tongue if you sucked them), always looked too big. I liked to feel his feet under the blue terry-towelling socks of the romper suits he wore, and I liked his small hands. He had spongy, curling baby hands with tiny nails. I would put my thumb on his palm to make his fingers fold unthinkingly, like the tentacles of a sea anemone, around it.

He was unlucky. When he was four, he was hospitalised with pneumonia. The next year, when all the kids on our street were jumping off our front verandah using umbrellas and plastic bags as parachutes, Alexander broke his arm. A few years later he cycled into a parked car and split his head open. He got the worst acne and was the only one in our family to grow heavy with puppy fat. He had strange, stiff, wiry hair, and he sucked his thumb until he was twelve.

He was sweet, though. As soon as he could walk and talk he would fetch Patrick and me food, ask Mum for favours on our behalf and, because he hated conflict, take the blame when we were in trouble.

Although his hands were barely big enough to hold a pair of scissors he insisted, and we insisted, that he had cut holes in Mum's good pair of togs, favourite umbrella and most of the hats on the hatstand. To end a two-hour standoff between kids and parents, which meant we couldn't eat dinner, Alexander voluntarily took the blame for putting a heel-shaped hole in the wall, but he couldn't tell our parents how it had happened, because he hadn't done it. It was Patrick who had slipped and put his foot through the particleboard.

Patrick and I set him tests of strength and he agreed to them all, no matter how cruel. One wet summer he stood under the mango tree at dusk with his shirt off, so we could count how many mosquitoes landed on his chest and back. Although he was afraid of heights, we convinced him to walk across a thin railing two metres above the ground because the first time he'd done it he'd slipped and caught himself, and he had looked like an acrobat: this gave our circus game authenticity. When we invited him to drink concoctions of Tabasco and chicory essence, he did it unquestioningly. Afterwards he'd cry, but he would never dob on us.

When he was really little, about two or three, he rolled down our driveway on a fraying plastic Fisher Price tricycle with a blue dump bucket at the back and crunched his forehead on a stone retaining wall. The cut was deep and needed stitches, so we were all stuffed into the white Nimbus and driven to my great-uncle Brian's house.

Great-uncle Brian was a GP, and at the front of his house was a clinic where he took ants out of our ears, examined our snot and let us listen to his stethoscope.

Mum and Dad left Patrick and me in the waiting room while Uncle Brian stitched up Alexander's head in the surgery. We read Spot and bickered.

Eventually all four of them came out, Alexander perched on Dad's hip and his forehead stitched up with blue thread. 'He didn't cry once,' Dad said. 'Even when the stitches were going in he just lay there. He's tough.'

Alexander was a beautiful child. Both my brothers were.

They had Mum's beauty: thick blond hair, huge eyes, small brown freckles and wicked smile. It was straightforward, there were no sharp lines or pronounced curves, but it was enough that people stopped to stare and comment. The boys got in trouble a lot, but because of their faces they got out of trouble a lot, too.

My brothers and I shouted, kicked, punched, hair-pulled, slapped, scratched and bit our way through childhood. Our shins were always covered in bruises and cuts. But while Patrick and I cried and demanded attention, Alexander just got on with what he was doing. This trait was what made us love him the most, and was also, in some ways, his most unlucky feature.

Patrick was talented at sports, I did well at school and Alexander wasn't good at anything much that he let on. He was inscrutable, and because of that he was clever at getting things done in his own way.

When I was five and Patrick two, Dad got rid of our television. Because of this, in the afternoons we went down to the park and mucked about on the little plank that stuck out through the mangroves, or to the house across the road where they had a trampoline, or next door, to Bert's workshop, where we could play with the offcuts and sawdust. We walked home from school and, when the tide was out, we took off our shoes and schlepped around in the creek bed looking for mudskippers and seeing how far we could make it before the water got deep again. But mostly we went to other people's houses to watch television.

At around 3.30 the Sorensen kids watched the ABC. We went to their house at least a couple of afternoons each week. The Sorensens had a long sectional couch and a white cat, Casper, who once got stuck in the roof for three days and lived.

At six, our next-door neighbours Marg and Bert ate dinner and watched *I Love Lucy* on the small black-and-white portable in their kitchen. Marg and Bert bought collectible porcelain dolls through the TV liftout and harvested rainwater in wheelie bins. Their whole household died a few months apart. First Bert broke his leg, lay down and didn't get up again, then Shadow the black dog died, then Marg died because she missed Bert.

But this was long before grief took them all. This was when Marg wore a tunic embroidered with pale-blue beads out dancing on Saturday afternoons. Slightly before she ordered a flower-print ironing-board cover, and was sent instead a cover with a full-length print of a man, naked except for a tool belt around his waist. It was around the time Bert built the greenhouse for his orchids, and made desks for Patrick and Alexander, whom he loved.

If we were quiet we could sneak out, climb the fence, squeeze through the dog hole and knock on the inside door. Marg was cranky when we interrupted dinner, but she made us warm Akta-Vite to drink at the kitchen table anyway.

On Saturday mornings we tiptoed up the back steps of the Heatleys' house, opened the door on the verandah—which was usually unlocked—walked through the Heatley parents' bedroom and into the living room where the Heatley kids were watching cartoons and eating rice bubbles. The Heatley kids were older than us. They taught us how pleasurable it was to throw socks at ceiling fans and took us can collecting under the stadium near our house when you could still exchange cans for money.

Occasionally Patrick and Alexander would get up early and go over to their house before anyone was awake. One morning when the sun hadn't been up long, and Susie and Bill were taking advantage of the quiet, Susie looked down and saw them walk past on their way to the living room. Patrick paused to say hello, then he and Alexander carried on to the living room.

The year that my aunt's friend Angela lived in the flats next door was the best. She made us all Vegemite toast and let us watch TV whenever we wanted.

To get out of the house we had to develop subterfuge. One trick was to yell, 'We're going, Mum,' and run out the door before she could ask us where. The best was to leave without saying anything.

One year for Christmas, Susie Heatley bought Mum a school bell so she could ring it when she wanted us to come home.

'I think I heard the bell ringing,' Susie or Mrs Sorensen would say. 'It's time for the Muir children to go home.'

'I didn't hear it,' Patrick would reply.

Often Mum would come out to find us. Then we stayed quiet, and if we were lucky she started talking to the other parent and we could continue to watch TV.

Maybe this was how Alexander learnt how to get things done without being noticed. Except, when he was thirteen, he stopped sneaking out to watch television during the day and started sneaking out at night to drink alcohol on the netball courts near our house. I didn't know this until after he died and, when I found out, I was surprised. It didn't fit with the version of him I had in my head.

But maybe my version of Alexander stalled at a certain point. Maybe I wanted to keep him the way I loved him most: strange and sweet, with a hand that fitted into mine, and a thumb that was pruney from being sucked.

I read Ben Okri's novel *The Famished Road* not long after Alexander died. The main character is an *abiku*, a Nigerian spirit child. The *abiku* are born to earthly families and live with them for a short while, until the other spirit children tempt them back to the land of the dead. An *abiku* in the family is bad luck, because they're sure to break your heart. I wondered if Alexander was something similar. It always seemed magical to me that he existed, and that he existed with us.

My grandma once described a family dinner she was at with my two brothers and some of their friends. 'Patrick can command a table,' she concluded, 'but even though Alexander is quieter, people just love him.'

And they did. The summer he left school he went to live with an aunt. I remember listening to a message she left on the answering machine telling our mum what a great kid he was. She sounded excited, as if she had only just realised it and had to relay the discovery. Then there was the teacher who wrote my dad a letter to say Alexander was one of the nicest students he'd taught.

And there was the way, when he was at the dinner table, he wouldn't say much, but everyone would gravitate towards him, so by the end of the night there would be two little cousins on either side of him and one on his lap. And every time he did say something, people would lean in close. If you were sitting at the end of the table farthest from him you could see the people at his end start to laugh, and people down your end would start saying 'What?' and the joke would be relayed from person to person until the whole table was laughing.

I miss Alexander's hands. I miss the way he ran up the stairs when he got home, the odd noises he was always making, his dumb hair and his chipped front teeth. I miss finding the pictures of block men with big mouths he drew on the old kitchen table, our placemats, the backs of envelopes and his desk. I miss the way he sang falsetto in the toilet and dressed up in Grandma's clothes to make us laugh.

I miss his head resting on my shoulder when he fell asleep on a long car trip. I miss how he was always happy: even though he went to swimming training almost every morning through summer and only ever made the relay team; even though his football team hardly ever won a game; even though, if he stopped his car at a red light, it wouldn't start again until he opened the bonnet and bashed the engine with a broom that he kept in his boot for this purpose.

I miss talking to him. I moved to Melbourne when I was twenty-one, and he was always the person I called when I was sad or lonely. He made me laugh, or he put my problems into perspective. He was unflappable, he didn't care what other people thought and, despite the teenage chaos that was sometimes around him, he had a stillness that I found comforting.

Almost exactly a year after Alexander died, Mum, Dad, Patrick and I finally cleaned out his room. My family isn't sentimental about objects. We sorted and discarded ruthlessly. The only things we kept were his trophies, some of his clothes and his books. Among the items that were thrown out was a pack of flash cards with handwritten Spanish phrases on the front and English phrases on the back.

'Should I keep these?' Dad said when he found them in a desk. Mum looked at them and shook her head.

'They're no use to him now,' she said, so Dad threw them in the bin.

It was rubbish day the next day. When he got home from work that night, Dad stopped the car to pull the bins in. Next to the recycling bin was one of Alexander's Spanish cards. He bent down to pick it up.

The card had fallen with the Spanish phrase up. 'Lo siento,' it read. Dad flipped it over. On the other side were the words 'I am sorry.'

It was an accident, but when Dad told us he was animated and his voice was shaky.

A few days later I was at my parents' house looking for a pair of earrings in my old room. There was an antique dresser in one corner, an heirloom, and I was pulling open drawers and rifling through the contents. The final drawer was only little; it had space for about two ring boxes, nothing more. I couldn't remember ever having used it, but I opened it anyway. Inside was a folded piece of ripped yellowing scrapbook paper. On the side facing up were two words written with felt-tipped pen in Alexander's muddy handwriting: 'Lo siento.'

I sat down on the bed and stared out the window until the sick feeling subsided.

3

WHEN WE WERE YOUNG

We grew up on a dead-end street in an inner-city suburb. At the southern end, next to a thin horse-paddock, was a sluggish, muddy creek, obscured by dark-green mangroves. Faded creaming-soda cans and Paddle Pop wrappers caught in the aerial roots that stuck out of its dark mud banks, sharp, and dense as tongue papillae.

The creek had its own smell—sweet and dirty—of hot clay, silt, sulphur, horseshit, eucalypt, grass seed, ducks, brackish water and mould. It was the smell of our childhood, and as I got older it was stultifying. To a teenager, the dead-end street was a cage.

I wanted to touch boys, and crack the thick rind of guilt, boredom and frustration wrapped tight around my life, under which everything worth doing bubbled. Drinking seemed the quickest route to dissolving my shyness.

For as long as I could remember Mum had warned us about alcohol. 'Your dad's side of the family can't drink, and my side of the family can drink too well,' she would say. She was one of twelve children. When she was young, they would peel wine labels off bottles and paste them to the cellar walls with their father.

My grandfather was a big man with a white moustache and soft white hair that ran in finger waves across his scalp. He was irascible and intelligent, charming and divisive. He adored women and children as people to be petted, was wary of teenagers, and respected men. We called him Papim. He called us woofy farts.

When Papim visited from Adelaide he started reading Mum's stash of Mills & Boons or Harlequins, and drinking whisky, at eleven in the morning. He didn't stop, except to nap in the afternoon.

If Papim was on the piss, which he often was, he was happy, funny and loud. Then he was cross. If he was cross, he yelled at Granny and the whole room flinched, aside from Granny, who ignored him. One evening when we were putting the dishes away she said to me: 'Never marry a man who drinks.'

The only thing Papim loved as much as drinking was driving, so he never stayed long. He grew tired of Mum's cooking and us, so he packed Granny into the car again and they drove south or west, along circuitous routes, with no stopping except for toilets. Sometimes it was the two of them. Other times they took friends or one of their children.

Mum was with Papim in the few days before he died. He couldn't drink, and she thought he was probably going through withdrawal. He could feel imaginary ants crawling up his body and was having convulsions.

During his eulogy my aunt told a story that had been told to her by some of his friends. My grandfather was at a formal party. In the early hours of the morning, when he was too pissed to walk straight, he got into his car to drive himself home.

After fumbling around for a while he was approached by a police officer, who asked him, politely, if he was okay.

My grandfather looked up at the policeman and said, 'I'm very glad you're here, officer, because someone has stolen my steering wheel.'

The policeman looked at him and said, 'You're in the back-seat, sir.'

This was long after we had left home, but Mum's warnings didn't make a difference anyway.

The first time I got drunk was in a friend's bedroom while we got ready for a dance. We shared a bag of Fruity Lexia between four of us, pouring it into plastic cups and, as we got drunker, sucking from the black plastic spout. It was sweet, which was our only requirement for alcoholic beverages. We stopped intermittently to assess each other's level of drunkenness, getting more and more giggly, falling off the bed, drawing eyeliner up our eyelids, snatching the goon bag from one another, discussing ways to hide our state so that we would be composed enough to enter the dance without being caught.

We woke up more tired than usual the next day, but that

was all. When you're fifteen you have to drink a lot to get a hangover.

When Alexander was fifteen he was arrested for the first time. He was drunk and breaking into cars with a couple of other friends to steal mobile phones and loose change when the police came. Alexander's friends ran, but he had just had a knee operation and could only limp. He hobbled down the road and tried to hide behind a tree. It was there that the cops found him.

Patrick and I were incredulous, not that he had been arrested, but that he had tried to avoid notice by standing behind a tree, which everyone knows from days of playing hide-and-seek is an amateur hide. I didn't think about how what he had done was stupid and irresponsible and an abuse of privilege: had Alexander needed money or a phone, he could have just asked. Instead I felt slightly proud. He had an aura of outlaw glamour. A few years later I would boast that 'I was the only child in my family who hadn't been arrested,' as if it were some great feat.

Some months after the incident with the cars there was a knock on the side door around 10 a.m. I was the only one home and just getting out of bed. There were two men standing on the small porch outside. They flashed badges at me and told me they were detectives from the nearby police station. One had his right trouser leg rolled up slightly to make room for the fat handgun strapped to his ankle. They were looking for Alexander.

'He's not here,' I told them.

The men were politely intimidating. They stood with legs apart and hands clasped. They questioned me about Alexander's movements the previous night.

'He was at home,' I told them. 'It was a school night.'

They told me there'd been an incident and Alexander was a suspect. Their questioning was persistent and repetitive, and the ankle gun was unnecessarily threatening on a weekday morning in a suburban street.

'Well, he was here last night,' I said again. 'But he's at school now.' Finally they were satisfied and I watched them go back down the driveway to their unmarked car.

One Christmas, I took a morning flight back to Brisbane. Mum picked me up and, when I got home, I went into Alexander's room to wake him up. There was a court order unfolded on his bed.

'What's this?' I asked.

'Nothing. Don't tell Mum,' he replied.

Later in that holiday Patrick, Alexander and I were sitting around talking. Paddy told us how lucky he was. He'd been driving from a friend's house to a footy field in suburban Brisbane with a bunch of mates in the back of his ute. There was an esky full of beer on the tray and everyone was drinking. The footy field was about five minutes from this friend's house, and he was a minute away when he heard a siren.

Paddy pulled over and wound down his window. In the side mirror he could see an irate cop walking towards him.

The cop came level with the driver's side door. 'Do you know how many rules you're breaking right now?' he said.

'I know. I'm sorry, officer.' Paddy said he thought he was gone. He said a friend of his who had been arrested for a serious offence, and whose case was still going through the courts, was sitting on the ute tray getting ready to bail. 'Peter was going to run. Then the cop came back and I was like, This is it. I am absolutely fucked.' The cop came up to the window. 'Mate, this is the luckiest day of your life.'

'He'd run out of tickets. I couldn't believe it! He couldn't do anything.' The cop told Patrick if he ever saw him breaking the law again he'd lock him up, but that hardly mattered. 'It was one of the best afternoons of my life,' Patrick said. He and his mates continued to the footy field, drank beer, kicked the ball and laughed at their fortune.

We were outside at the square wooden table on the back deck. It was summer and the frangipani tree was fragrant with rotting flowers. Alexander laughed. 'I am so unlucky,' he said.

He told us he had been out the week before. It was midnight and he was walking home from the pub. He was crossing a park when he realised he had to wee urgently.

He found a bush that he thought was in the middle of the park, unzipped his fly, pulled down his undies and started to wee on it. 'I was standing there when I heard a siren and I thought, Oh, fuck. I looked around and I could see a cop car, with its lights and sirens and everything, headed towards me. Then this cop opens the door and she was yelling at me, asking me what the hell I was doing. I was like, "I'm doing a wee. I just needed to do a wee."'

I can imagine him, my tall shaggy-haired brother, standing next to the dark bush with his pants down, the look of surprise on his face. Fleetingly contemplating the unlikelihood of the situation before being shoved into the car and taken to the station.

'They charged me with indecent exposure and took my fingerprints,' Alexander said. As usual, Patrick and I were indignant. 'For weeing? They fingerprinted you? That's crazy.'

Apart from Papim, we weren't really exposed to drunkenness when we were growing up. My parents had a glass of wine at dinner each night and cognac on Fridays. Sometimes when we were little, if we were at a barbecue and he was drinking it, Dad let us have a sip of his beer and we told him it was disgusting. Most kids I knew were allowed to have a sip of their parents' drinks at some point, and most had the same reaction.

When I was seventeen my mum gave me two light beers to take to a party—it was the only time she ever gave me alcohol when I was underage. This was common practice among parents at the time. 'At least if I give these to you I know what you're drinking,' she said. I had been drinking for years by then—two light beers was a paltry amount. I accidentally dropped them on the way in to the party, so I shared some bottles of Passion Pop with a friend instead.

If we wanted to drink we stole wine from my parents' stash or arranged for someone's older sibling to buy it for us. Other kids tried their luck at the bottle shop or got a fake ID.

I don't know why it was so important that there was alcohol, always. To go without just seemed to not be an option. Without it, I would rub up against the elements of the world, and chafe and blister. With it, everything was softer, easier. You had a drink and you slid into nonchalance and from there into conversations and new situations and adventures and forgetfulness.

My brothers and I were different, but people who knew us

sometimes remarked that our familial similarities were evident when we were drunk. We seemed to go slightly further than everyone else.

One night a couple of years ago Patrick told me he could trace 'pretty much every problem in his life' back to drinking. 'But I enjoy it. I enjoy it so much that sometimes…' He paused. 'I should stop drinking, because of the problems that stem from it, but I just enjoy it.'

'I feel the same,' I said, excitedly, as though we had just discovered matching star-shaped moles on our thumbs. 'It's the same for me, too.'

On my desk is *On Booze*, a compendium of F. Scott Fitzgerald's writings on drinking. It's lying face down next to a cup of coloured felt pens and broken plaster fragments I mean one day to glue back together. The pull quote on the book's back cover is, 'First you take a drink, then the drink takes a drink, then the drink takes you.' This makes sense to me.

4

THE MORNING AFTER

I lost my virginity when I was seventeen in a flimsy prefab house in an inland suburb on the Gold Coast. The house had beige tiles and white walls. It was cheap, it wouldn't age well, but it looked modern, and it was clean. It contained functional objects—an ironing board, a surfboard, a drying rack and a mattress without sheets. There were no knick-knacks. The only decorative flourishes were surfing posters Blu-Tacked to the walls—a squint-eyed man barrelling down a wave, a soft-eyed woman in a sandy bikini.

I woke up naked, drunk and alone on a mattress on the floor of one of the bedrooms. I was sleeping next to a built-in wardrobe with mirrored doors, and on the small window on the opposite wall there was a dark-blue curtain with no underlay. It was just after sunrise, and the dim watery light coming through the window coverings made it seem as if I was in a submarine in shallow water, or the lower berth of a ship.

Diagonally across from me was a single bed. There was a lump in the bed. It groaned, rolled over and looked at me. 'You're awake,' it said. 'You wouldn't let me sleep with you—you kicked me out.'

I shut my eyes and went back to sleep.

Twenty minutes later I woke up again. It was awake, too.

'Did we…?' I started asking, and he answered before I finished.

'Yes. You said no at first, but then you said it was okay. Was it really your first time?'

'Mm. Was there, um, did you use…'

'Yep, don't worry.'

'I don't know your name.'

'It's Greg.'

Greg was a potbellied nurse seven years older than me. The only way I could corroborate his story was through a detached, brief memory—only a few seconds long—of him grunting and puffing on top of me. And my vagina was sore. I couldn't see a condom anywhere.

'Where are we?' I said.

'At my house.'

'Can you take me back to my friend?'

It was January 2001, the holidays before I started university. The previous afternoon my friend and I had caught the train down to the Gold Coast to hang out with a guy she'd met at Schoolies. He was eight years older than us: a tradie and a small-time drug dealer. One of these was a lucrative business. His car was new. His recently constructed house was furnished with Balinese carvings, architectural plants and small stone temples.

He picked us up from Surfers Paradise. On the way to his place, he stopped off to buy my friend and me a bottle of tequila, and himself a few cartons of beer.

My friend was tiny and pretty, with platinum-blond hair and an eating disorder. When she was seventeen, she attracted handsome, predatory older men who had well-defined muscles. Her face was always coated in thick make-up and, from the point where her school dress ended to where her knicker line began, she slashed mad, thin horizontal stripes with a box cutter. The cuts got itchy as they healed and she compulsively rubbed her palms along her pants or skirt to scratch them.

At school she moved between her mother's house and the house where her dad lived with his new family, not belonging in either. After school she moved with her boyfriend into his dad's house. The dad lived with his new wife and newer children; he didn't want his older sons there, so he kicked the boyfriend, my friend and the boyfriend's little brother out, and they moved into a warehouse the dad owned. The warehouse was bleak. It was next to a train line on an industrial back street in one of Brisbane's flat, dusty outer suburbs, round the corner from a dirty strip mall.

My friend left that boyfriend periodically and moved into her mother's house or her ex-boyfriend's house or, once, into my parents' house. Her car was always packed with stuff because she never knew where she would sleep. The last time I saw her she was living downstairs at her grandma's and she was happy because she finally had a bookshelf.

My friend was smart and funny and sad. She worked hard for everything and she didn't think she was good at anything. But her explosive, unpredictable relationships seemed impossibly romantic to me.

In high school I dated a boy who folded each item of clothing as he took it off. He hung up his jacket and rolled up his socks while I lay fully clothed on his single bed and waited for him to join me in polite, vanilla cavorting. He got straight high distinctions and my parents loved him. He drove me where I wanted to go, all the while providing informed, stimulating conversation on politics, psychology or philosophy, punctuating the serious parts with sweet, silly puns.

When I broke up with him, my father said to me, only partially in jest, 'You've just lost the best thing that will ever happen to you.' But I wanted to have explosive affairs with shady part-time criminals, not parent-sanctioned relationships with potential marriage material. Although the boy and I said we'd keep in touch, we soon fell out of contact. I didn't mind.

A few weeks after my high-school relationship ended, I stood in the part-time drug dealer's kitchen while men in their early twenties came in twos and threes through the door, until there were eight or nine of us standing around the bench. I was anxious, excited and unable to speak. The part-time dealer lined up tequila shots, lemon pieces and a salt cellar. My friend and I had one shot, then another, and another, until the bottle was half empty. The liquor sizzled and cauterised my nerves so that my stupid, shy tongue could form words. The alcohol tamped down my hunger, too: I had only eaten breakfast.

We were the centre of a sly attention. Currents of conversation excitingly thick with innuendo whirled around us and, except for the occasional quick, appraising glance, my friend and I were deliberately excluded. Someone rolled a joint. My friend said loudly, 'Do that thing, Elspeth.'

'What thing?' I asked.

'You know, the boob thing.'

I had recently discovered I could make my breasts move independently of one another; to make my friend laugh, I would move them in time to the beat of whatever song we were listening to.

'Really?' I said.

'Yes, do it!'

'What thing?' one of the men asked.

'She makes her boobs dance to music. It's hilarious.'

One of the men started baying. 'Do it, come on. Please, do it.' The others joined in: 'Come on. Please! Show us!'

'Okay,' I said, and they bayed.

My lack of artfulness at seventeen is impossible, now, for me to understand. I couldn't comprehend anyone else not thinking like me, like my friend, like Brisbane private-school girls. It was nothing at all to me, this absurd little action. It was not sexual—it was funny. My breasts, like my fingers or my hair, were just my body. I knew my post-pubescent self had a power that my pre-pubescent self did not, and sometimes, then, I exploited people's interest in it and, later, I exploited it a lot, but it was also embarrassing and annoying.

Perhaps some of those men also thought it was funny. But I think, too, the action set me up as an exhibit—an interactive exhibit. I still had my T-shirt on but, even so, women who got wasted and directed attention to their tits were asking for it. I was a puzzle, a warm-meat puzzle.

I wasn't entirely unaware of the type of attention I was attracting. I was interested in sex, too. Probably just as interested in it as they were. I remember some of them were kind of cute, although I don't remember their names, faces or what they were wearing.

I remember Greg. He was short and seemed older than the other men. I remember him because I had singled him out as the person I was least attracted to. He was a friend of the part-time dealer's housemate, and I felt slightly sorry for him. While the other men there were hard and handsome, funny and edgy, he was plain and quiet and a little bit chubby. Although the others pretended to ignore my friend and me, he openly gazed at us from the back of the group, his right hand gripping a beer in a stubby cooler, a small smile on his face.

When I finished the men clapped, and my friend laughed and poured me a shot. We drank the bottle of tequila quickly. Soon after my memory goes blank, except for three clear flashes—sitting on a chair in the driveway of the party house eating a piece of white bread, walking naked down a hallway, and being squashed underneath him, his breath in my face.

When Greg and I got into his car so he could drive me back

to the house it was still early—before eight. 'I just wanna check the surf,' he said. I nodded. He drove fast along a smooth curved road. I didn't speak, and he spoke nervously.

'This is the Gold Coast Indy track,' he said, slipping a CD into the player. It was Something For Kate's *Echolalia*. Everyone was listening to it that summer.

The morning surf was beautiful. Long clean waves moved in slow motion towards the shore, which was unusually empty. There was breeze enough to cut the first heat of the day, but not too much to pull goose pimples from my skin. I sat in the car with the window down and waited while he walked along the foreshore pavement as if the morning were like any other, and not the morning after the night I had sex for the first time.

I used to fall over a lot when I was a kid. During the descent I usually had two strong emotions. The first was horror at the coming pain. This occurred when there was still a small hope that I might regain my footing. The second, which happened closer to impact, when there was no point struggling against the inevitable, was apathy. In my tequila fog I felt the second emotion, only at its centre was a small, hard nub of sadness. I fucked up, I thought.

Greg slid back into the driver's seat. 'Good, eh?' he said, and started the car.

We drove in silence back to the house. When we arrived he turned to me. 'Can I have your number?'

I shook my head and got out of the car.

He followed me inside. 'I'm just gonna see John for a sec,' he said.

'I don't know where my friend is,' I said.

'Come and ask John. He'll know.'

I followed him to a room at the back of the house. John was lying on his bed. When he saw us, he grinned. 'So, that's where you are. You disappeared. Looks like you two had a good night, eh?'

I smiled too hard. 'Um, do you know where my friend is?'

'Yeah, she's in the other bedroom. It's just down the hall.'

'Okay, thanks.'

'See ya,' said Greg.

'Yep,' I said.

—

At Catholic school, our sex education wasn't expansive. Apparently there was a class where our Physical Education teacher showed everyone how to put a condom on a cucumber, but I wasn't there. There was no mention of gay sex, masturbation, abortion, that the desire to fuck was healthy and mutual, that a woman's sex drive is just as strong as a man's, that sex could be fun.

At the end of Grade Twelve we were shown a video of an American evangelist railing against sex before marriage. 'But he said he loved me,' she whined in a scathing imitation of all those girls left pregnant and unmarried by opportunistic men.

Sex was something men tried to sneak out of you; if you were stupid enough to open your legs before you had a ring on your finger, you were a slut. The video was widely regarded as a joke, but it was an extreme example of how we were protected and infantilised by our parents and teachers.

Dads joked about vetting boyfriends, jocularly noting that 'they'd better watch themselves.' We were called 'princesses' or 'little princesses', and we needed to be 'taken care of or else', as if the only reason we might have sex was if it were pushed onto us against our will.

I was sixteen the first time I realised that my body was a problem. I was staying with my family at the beach and I wanted to go out at night with my friend to buy an ice cream. We were only allowed out if we were accompanied by one of my brothers. I had been responsible for them throughout my childhood and now they were in charge of protecting my safety. I was furious and ashamed.

—

I walked into the room where my friend was, to find her in bed with the guy she'd met at Schoolies. 'Well, I just lost my virginity to half a bottle of tequila,' I said.

Later, when the part-time dealer went to the toilet, I whispered, 'I don't know if we used a condom.' And when he had to go outside to make a phone call, I said: 'Could we go now? I think maybe I need to get the morning-after pill.'

'Really—now?'

'Yeah. I just, um, I...'

'No, it's fine, sweetie—let's go.'

The part-time drug dealer dropped us off at Robina Station, and we sat on the empty platform with our eyes screwed up against the glare and our legs stretched out in front of us so we made sagging arcs. I held my throbbing head in my hands.

'Was it okay?' my friend asked.

I shrugged. 'I don't know—I don't really remember.'

'Oh, honey.'

'Do you know where I can go for, to get…'

'There's a clinic in the Valley. They give the morning-after pill out for free,' she said.

'Can you come with me?'

'Sure.'

I felt like shit on the train. We both dozed and when we got into the city she said, 'Okay, I'm going to meet Julia. I'll call you about going to the clinic.'

I messaged her a few hours later and she messaged back: 'Oh sweetie, I totally forgot. Did you still want me to come? I was going to go home, I'm really shattered.' And I wrote: 'Sure, don't worry,' because I didn't want to make a big deal about it when her sexual escapades were much more frequent and daring.

I called a friend and told her what had happened. 'Do you think maybe you should tell your mum?' she said.

'No.'

'I think maybe you should go with someone to the clinic,' she said, 'and I'm not in Brisbane at the moment.' It was summer holidays and everyone was at the beach. 'Just tell her.'

I went into my parents' bedroom, where Mum was reading a book. 'Mum, something happened last night. Please don't tell Dad,' I begged.

She was sad and worried, and the worry made her angry. 'What do you want to do?'

'I need to get the morning-after pill. There's a clinic in Fortitude Valley. Can you take me there?'

'Do you need to make an appointment?'

'I don't know—I don't think so—I think you can just walk in.'

Mum called and made an appointment anyway. 'Get in the car,' she said.

We drove for a while in silence, then she said: 'Who was the man?'

'Just a guy. I don't know. I don't remember very well.'

We had to wait. The waiting room was small and shabby, but comfortable, and warm in the afternoon sun. There were tabloid magazines five months old scattered on the cheap padded suites with metal arms, and a water cooler in the corner. On the walls were posters about AIDS and chlamydia tests.

I was scared that the pill was going to give me a migraine, and ashamed. I couldn't believe I was at a sexual-health clinic with my mum.

A sweet doctor with peppery hair called me through and examined me. At the end of the consultation she gave me the pill in a packet and told me the correct way to take it. Then she said, 'Do you want to press rape charges?'

I was horrified. 'No,' I replied and shook my head. 'It was my fault. I was drunk. I said it was okay. It was my fault.'

'Okay,' she said, and sighed.

The extent to which I'd been complicit with the man was hazy. I could easily believe I'd revoked my initial refusal, if just to keep the peace. Years of being trained to be polite, be nice, be pretty, smile (*you're so much prettier when you smile*), do what you're told, don't talk back, had made this kind of reaction automatic. Without full control of my faculties, I was unlikely to second-guess it.

I had been drunk. If I had put myself in a state where I couldn't control what I was doing, I reasoned, I only had myself to blame for being taken advantage of.

I didn't blame the nurse for taking advantage of me, because he was drunk, too, so how could he have properly understood my wishes, especially when my consent was ambiguous?

Because I didn't have the language to discuss what had happened, I buried the experience away or laughed it off: 'I lost my virginity to half a bottle of tequila,' I told people if the topic ever came up in conversation.

The experience wasn't horrific. I wasn't injured, impregnated or infected. I wasn't intimidated or harassed, made to feel afraid or purposefully humiliated. But I felt used. And because what happened didn't align with my understanding of sexual assault, instead of being angry at the person who used me I was ashamed of myself. I thought I was a person worth not very much, and this notion fed into my relationships, which in my early twenties were short, angry and chaotic.

5

CANDY IS DANDY

Fifteen years later, Greg's actions are clearer to me. He took me away from the party and my friend. He drove, which suggests he was sober enough to navigate the road; his judgement wasn't entirely impaired. I was in his house, in a location I didn't know; I was in his power. I initially said no to sex, and he knew it was my first time. Although he told me I said yes, I was sufficiently intoxicated not to remember this. I didn't consent freely. I kicked him out of the bed once he'd finished—I didn't want him to touch me.

Greg mirrored a type of offender profiled in the 2010 Australian Institute of Family Studies report into sexual assault, *Giving Voice*. Women who had been sexually assaulted under the influence of alcohol or drugs regularly reported that they had no romantic or sexual interest in the perpetrator. Often they thought he was a loser. The perpetrator was framed as someone who used alcohol to overcome social barriers that might otherwise hinder his ability to interact with women. Whether the assault was 'opportunistic' or 'planned', the perpetrator generally used a combination of 'trust, social norms, control, alcohol and surprise' to incapacitate, isolate and place his own desires onto the victim, as well as to control the interaction. When alcohol affected the victim's memory, perpetrators reframed the version of events to appear normal and consensual.

Australian and overseas research has found that alcohol is a factor in half of all sexual assaults. While this is inconclusive—it's not known, for instance, what is the *role* of alcohol in sexual assault—it's still alarming. A 2014 *Lancet* journal study found that sixteen in every hundred Australian and New Zealand women older than fifteen have experienced sexual assault at the hands of someone other than their partner—more than twice the global average.

My belief in my own culpability was based on rape myths about inappropriate female sexual behaviour and female drunkenness. As recently as two years ago a VicHealth survey found that one in five Australians believe a drunk woman is partly responsible for her rape.

At the end of 2013, in response to a report about the high rate of sexual assault on college campuses in America, the *Slate* columnist Emily Yoffe wrote an impassioned plea, 'College Women: Stop Getting Drunk'. Yoffe writes of her frustration at what she perceived to be society's inability to warn young women about the relationship between binge drinking and rape: 'A misplaced fear of blaming the victim has made it unacceptable to warn inexperienced young women that when they get wasted they are putting themselves in potential peril.'

Rebuttals were soon published on *Salon*, the *Wire*, *Jezebel* and even *Slate*—in a piece entitled 'To Prevent Rape on College Campuses Focus on the Rapists, Not the Victims', Yoffe's colleague Amanda Hess criticised her for not talking about the education of men as well as women.

But the article also met with praise. Sympathetic pieces ran in the *Washington Post* and the *Atlantic*. In Australia, Mia Freedman wrote on *Mamamia*: 'I'll tell [my daughter] that getting drunk when she goes out puts her at a greater risk of danger. All kinds of danger. I'll tell her that being drunk impairs your judgment, slows your reflexes and dramatically reduces your ability to assess risks and escape from harm.'

It was clear that Yoffe's article, and those that supported her reasoning, came from a place of concern. There have been many times in my life, including the night I lost my virginity, when I wished I had drunk less, because my actions would have been different, safer.

Yet Yoffe was reinforcing ideas that might stop women from recognising and reporting drunken sexual assault. Over the past few years I have asked a lot of people what they think has changed about how we drink: invariably one of the first, always concerned answers is, 'women drink more,' as though this signifies that something has gone wrong.

Anne Fox, an English anthropologist who studies drinking cultures, believes that the imperative to control sexuality rises from a need to ensure paternity. 'Alcohol,' she writes, 'enhances the sexual response in females by increasing testosterone; it reduces anxiety and makes faces more attractive; culturally, it is often associated with uninhibited behaviour—clearly, this is not a substance that is safe to have around in paternalistic societies that are dominated by the fear of female infidelity.'

There are plenty of Australian ad campaigns aimed at preventing drunken violence. The ads call on male perpetrators to 'Walk Away, Chill Out' or 'Stop Before It Gets Ugly' or 'Be a Real Man and Walk Away'. I haven't seen an Australian ad that confronts alcohol and rape.

Two of my closest female friends have been involved in forced sexual incidents. Both were drunk, and both had the experience with someone who they chose to go home with but decided against sleeping with. Each time the man kept mauling them after he'd been rebuffed. Neither woman reported the incident to the police—nor did they even think of doing so. One of them ran into the man who had assaulted her a few years later and described still feeling fear.

A former housemate of mine teaches circus tricks to children. She would do headstands on our kitchen floor, then pull her legs down into the splits so she looked like a hand-drawn 'T'. She could do chin-ups on the bar above the door that lead to the living room, ride a unicycle, walk on stilts and swing upside down on the trapeze. On weekends she was an acrobat and during the week she supplemented her income by life modelling. She farted and burped her way around the house, she started swearing at dawn, and her bedroom was full of plants in bottles; on every surface there was something growing.

At breakfast she would show me the bruises that dappled her skin. One was from the trapeze, one was from falling off stilts; that one was where her acrobat partner kicked the boil on her neck when climbing up to stand on her shoulders. She is funny, tough and brave.

She told me a story about her past one morning at the kitchen table. It was the last of the cool days and through the louvres I could see that the paperbark tree was beginning to bloom. In a few weeks eastern rosellas would hang by their beaks from the yellow flowers during the day and flying foxes would fight in the branches at night, making a noise like water draining through a blocked plughole. The jasmine vine outside my bedroom sagged under thousands of white blossoms, and the scent was pervasive; after a while I couldn't smell it anymore, except when the wind changed. On this morning the perfume blew into the kitchen and when I turned my head I got a full blast: sweetness, the promise of summer.

My housemate didn't drink much in high school. She still doesn't. There was alcoholism in her family and she wasn't interested in perpetuating it. She had decided not to go to Schoolies, to avoid the drinking; instead she was spending the week at a family friend's farm. She wanted to get away from her small town about an hour and a half's drive from Brisbane, and have some time to herself.

A few weeks before she finished school she was walking

home from a café when she met a man. They started talking and he asked her to come with him to the pub. He was twenty-six and she was seventeen. She went with him and he asked if he could buy her a drink. She refused and told him she didn't really drink, that there was alcoholism in her family. After the pub, they went back to the café. My housemate saw her friends and went over to sit with them.

Later in the evening, when the café was closing, the man came over to her table and asked her to come home with him. He said he would buy a bottle of wine on the way. She was shocked: he was nine years older than her and the proposition was brazen. She was confused that he'd offered to buy a bottle of wine when he knew she wasn't a drinker. She rebuffed him, and he seemed upset.

The next time she saw him was at the same café. He was there because his band was playing; she was celebrating a friend's twenty-first birthday. It was one of the rare occasions when she felt like drinking. Her friends were there and she reasoned it would be safe. She was an inexperienced drinker and soon on her way to being drunk.

She walked up to the man and said hello. She was tipsy and felt bad about the previous week. He was standoffish at first, but when he saw that she was drinking he started buying her drinks.

Her friends encouraged her to go home with him. She'd recently broken up with her boyfriend, the only person she'd slept with, and they thought it would be good for her to sleep with someone else. She went outside with the man. They kissed against a car and he tried to get his hand down her skirt. She pushed it away. He became angry, and she was distressed.

When they went back inside, her friends were gone. She thought maybe they had forgotten her because they were drunk, or they had decided she would be okay on her own.

The man suggested they go back to his house and they ended up in his bedroom, making out. There were books about Buddhism on the shelf at the end of his bed. They had only been kissing for a short while when he tried to take it further. She wasn't ready, and said so, but he didn't listen. She tried to pull away and he pushed her down.

'I was really confused at that point because I'd wanted to be there, but I'd never been treated like that by anyone before. I remember as time went past wanting to push him away more and more, and he would hold me down harder, and then at some stage I just froze and looked out the window hoping he would finish.'

He raped her repeatedly during the night. He was much bigger than her and she was terrified that if she fought back he would hurt her badly, so she lay still. In the morning he drove her home as if nothing had occurred. 'I was confused and unsure and didn't really know what had happened,' she told me.

My housemate decided to go through with her post-school plan to spend a couple of weeks at a family friend's farmhouse. But when she got there, the friend was out for the day.

'I was left in this house by myself out in the country. I really wanted to get back into town and get the morning-after pill. I was scared of getting pregnant because at one point during the night he was trying to have sex with me without a condom and I was trying to push him away, and I don't know if we used one or not. So my friend eventually drove me back. I couldn't tell him why I had to go back into town.'

I asked her why she didn't go to the police. 'I didn't think anyone would believe me. I had no proof. I told my friend, whose birthday it was that night, and she said: "I spoke to you the next day and you didn't say anything had happened." It was a small community and I knew that often women who said men raped or sexually assaulted them bore the brunt of the community's anger, not the other way around.'

Despite her experience, my housemate—my tough, no-bullshit friend—was concerned for the man who attacked her. She couldn't fathom his motives: she thought there must be something wrong with him. But ultimately she didn't go to the police because she hadn't fought back. 'I didn't think I had a case because I hadn't been broken. Sometimes the way that people speak about it is that women who fight back are brave or whatever, and people don't understand why women don't fight. I felt ridiculous that I didn't fight.'

6

WHISKY AND TOILET WATER

I moved to Melbourne two weeks after I turned twenty-one—when Patrick was eighteen and Alexander seventeen—and fell in love with it, hard. In Brisbane it felt like there was nothing to do, nowhere to walk, no place for anyone who didn't look like everyone else. I would catch a bus for hours to get to a suburb that was the same as the suburb before it and the one I'd come from. Everything old was periodically demolished to make way for the new, and the sun-bleached streets were dull and empty. Melbourne had kept its layers. Its tight, grimy alleyways were teeming with life.

I moved in with my best friend from school, Xochi. She lived in a flat that was once the servants' quarters of the last crumbling mansion on Albert Park Road, South Melbourne. The smeared windows were covered with second-hand sheets to prevent the office workers in the surrounding skyscrapers from looking in, and it was always cold, even in summer. There wasn't really enough space for another person in the flat, so we shared her bed.

Two other people lived with us. One was a sweet Colombian who worked as a cleaner in a hotel and wore chunky calf-high leather boots on Saturdays. He didn't speak much English, but his smile was heartbreaking. Every weekend he scrubbed the bath and, once, although he didn't take them himself, he brought home a bag of drugs he'd found at work to share. A friend who lived downstairs cut them up and arranged them in lines. After some deliberation, a volunteer was found to sniff them first. They turned out to be orange sherbet.

The other man was Australian, an artist with curly black hair and a beautiful face. I was in love with him, he was in love with Xochi, and she was in love with no one.

A month after I arrived contractors chopped down the trees outside the living room and Xochi said she didn't want to live there anymore because what was the point now the trees were gone.

We found a small dark flat in East St Kilda, a few doors down from a lamp shop that was never open. It was one of four flats in an Art Deco block named after an ugly Scottish castle. In the front yard were grim trees with leaves more grey than green, but in the backyard was a lemon tree; and if we stood on the roof of the garage during the day and looked towards the city we could see a synagogue; and if we stood in the same place at night, looked up, and were lucky, we would see space junk burning through the ozone.

There was no mobile reception in our flat, so a few times a week we used the payphone across the road to call our parents. In the streets near our house you could buy drugs and sex; sometimes, while we were talking on the phone, men stopped their cars to ask if we were working. We pointed at our oversized flannel pyjamas, Ugg boots and stained cardigans, and told them to fuck off. The sex workers put effort into their make-up and wore difficult clothes. Even when it was freezing they wore skirts that showed tight thighs and calves—bodies made lithe by walking, and standing for hours, in high heels. At night they took clients to the car park at the back of our building, and I lay awake listening to the cars drive in and out. It was so different from suburban Brisbane, where the main nocturnal sounds were non-human. I felt comforted to know that people were around and alive.

Anything we needed the city provided—free furniture on hard-rubbish days; intermittent work that was sometimes shitty and sometimes okay; cheap food, and places to drink.

Every couple of days Xochi and I bought a four-litre cask of red wine. Depending on how many people were staying, it took us one or two days to drink it, and then we would buy another. Because we were often drunk in the evenings it was difficult to do the housework and the dirty dishes piled up next to the sink, and on the table and the floor. The carpet was permanently encrusted with bicarbonate soda and salt to cover the red-wine stains, and there were burn marks from the time we tried to see if the chimney was blocked by lighting logs and pinecones in the fireplace, and a burning log rolled onto the carpet. Behind the couches were bits of old lettuce from a salad fight we never properly cleaned up.

Everything in our fridge was growing. A month before Christmas a friend found, at the back of the second shelf, an old sausage with a neon-green frill at least two and a half centimetres high.

Sometimes I fell asleep at my job in the afternoons. My salary lasted half a week, then I begged tram fares from itinerant sex buddies and ate packet noodles. I got an infection in my armpit, an open sore that I couldn't get rid of because I couldn't give up drinking for the three weeks required for antibiotics to work.

Between one and eight extra people stayed in our two-bedroom flat at any time—a tiny, forlorn schoolmate who scrubbed the floors on her hands and knees at night because she was pregnant and jetlagged and couldn't sleep; a friend without a place to live who, when she moved out, left the murderous goldfish that was in the end my most steadfast companion; an exquisite-looking Englishwoman of Thai origin who spoke like a chav and took drugs with B-grade Australian movie actors; an angry little American man who told us he found gold in a shoebox in his attic; passing bands; school friends; friends of friends; Xochi's brothers and sisters; Patrick and Alexander.

Sometimes the beautiful artist turned up before sunrise, crying and smoking cigarettes until Xoch let him in. They were sleeping together, and I was trying not to bail him up in the kitchen and make him too many cups of tea.

One night when we were rotten drunk I brought him water

in a blender so he wouldn't get too bad a hangover. He was thirsty and grateful and chugged it quickly, and I was happy until he started choking. The bottom of the blender was full of old mashed potato. But he just laughed and hugged me, and I loved him even more.

It was the most fun I had ever had. Every day was an adventure and each morning I woke up in a painful, joyful haze, lay in bed looking at the light filtering through the lemon tree, and the vine around my window, which was where the cockroaches lived, and wondered at my good luck.

At the end of that year, 2005, Xochi went to Canada on exchange for six months and I was desolate. The night before she left I fell down the stairs and one of my thighs turned the colour of a blood plum. In the morning I woke in Xochi's bed next to a bucket of vomit. Floating in the middle were a clock and two earrings. 'Where did that come from?' I asked.

'From you,' Xochi said. 'You pissed yourself, too.'

'No, I didn't.'

'Yes, you did.'

'Well, at least I didn't cry about you leaving.'

'You sobbed. You wouldn't stop.'

After Xoch left the artist did, too, and my friend since kindergarten replaced them. He moved in while I was at work; his mother flew down from Brisbane to help him, and when she saw our flat she cried. His sister said it looked like a crack den. He called me at work to ask if we'd ever defrosted the freezer. I told him I didn't think so, I didn't know you had to defrost freezers, but to chip through the ice with a butter knife and dislodge whatever he needed. That was what I usually did. Once, to my excitement, I had discovered some ancient Paddle Pops in the expanding berg.

Each day my friend would wake up and get dressed so he could look for a job, and each afternoon I would come home from work to find him sitting in the living room with half a bottle of wine or empty Smirnoff Black bottles, or both. 'I did mean to look for a job,' he would tell me. 'But the day just got away.'

'Oh, well—tomorrow,' I said, and we drank another bottle of wine, and another, and then we went out if we had any money.

Xochi was better at living than I was: without her my life cracked. I cobbled basic meals together for my friend and me out of pasta and packet noodles and shrivelled snow peas from the garden. I called the real estate to say the rent would be a week or two late. At work functions I learned to grab as much finger food as possible, enough to be uncomfortably full, and hope the feeling would last for a while. There wasn't enough money for phone credit, tram tickets, electricity bills, gas bills, or sometimes toothpaste, but there was always enough to get fucked up. Drugs were expensive, and tricky to get because their procurement needed to be planned in advance, but alcohol was cheap—five dollars for a cleanskin, ten for a cask—and there were bottle shops all around us, including a twenty-four-hour one a fifteen-minute walk away.

Every few weeks I phoned each of my brothers. I told them all the stories I chose not to tell my parents and they told me some of the stories they chose not to tell my parents.

Alexander had left school by then. Sometimes he told me stories about his drunken escapades, like the time he and his mates went to another friend's house after the races. There wasn't much furniture because the friend had only just moved in, but in the back room there was an esky with home-brand soft drink. They emptied the soft drink on the wooden floors and took their clothes off so they could slide around in the bubbles. Then they decided that one of the boys should sit on the esky lid and they would slide him around on the floor. They had been doing this for a few minutes when one of them noticed it was slightly darker in the room and looked up. A couple of cops were staring down at them.

'It must have looked strange to them,' Alexander said.

'Yes,' I agreed.

Other times, Alexander reassured me about life. He was thoughtful, and often strangely wise, wiser than me. 'What am I doing?' I would say sometimes. He never asked those types of questions.

'Don't worry, El. You'll figure it out.' He was working in a pathology lab then, and a colleague of his in her thirties had just decided what she wanted to study. He told me about her. 'See,' he said. 'People just do things at different times.'

The block of apartments sold and we got notice to move out. My friend moved back to Brisbane. A girl I barely knew, a friend of a friend, moved in. Annaliese—Anna—was supposed to stay for a few weeks, just enough time to find somewhere else to live. At the same time the tiny English girl who had been living in the sunroom moved out and her friend, a chef with an East London accent, moved in.

The chef was affected by alcohol in a way I haven't seen since. He was sober three times—the day we met him, the day he moved out and once on his way to the shower. He moved into the flat on a Wednesday and on the Thursday morning around 4 a.m. he came home with his taxi driver and they partied until dawn. In the morning I went into the living room and found him passed out on the carpet. On my way out I went back in to check on him. He was gone, and there was a big piss stain where he had been lying.

That night Anna phoned. 'Can you come home? The chef's gone crazy.'

When I arrived at the flat she opened the door before I could get my key out. 'I think he's in the sunroom,' she whispered.

We walked quietly into the kitchen. I turned to Anna and whispered, 'What happened?'

'I was sitting on the couch. He walked through the living room to go to the shower and he was fine. We had a completely normal conversation,' she said. 'He must have been drinking in the shower, because when he came back through his eyes were glassy and he was swaying. He saw me, dropped his towel and just stood there, naked. I left the room, but he's still in there.'

'What do you want to do?'

'I don't know. I think he's going out.'

We cooked dinner and went outside to eat it. The temperature had been above thirty degrees for a few days and the air was still. The guy who lived upstairs came down for a beer. We told him about the chef. He told us about the coffee he'd made himself that morning. 'I thought it tasted strange. It was, like, kind of meaty or something,' he said. 'When I pulled the plunger up to throw out the grounds I saw four soggy cockroaches.'

They had come out of the vine on the back wall, he explained.

I put my beer down and retched.

Anna looked up. 'Oh, fuck,' she said, and pointed to the kitchen. The chef was swaying past the kitchen table, making his way outside.

He sat down. 'Hi,' I said.

Anna was silent.

The chef said to the man from upstairs: 'Everyone wants me, but they can't have me.'

'I think you should go to bed,' the man from upstairs replied.

The chef turned to Anna. 'You want me, but you can't have me.'

'I don't want you,' she said, half laughing.

Anna, the man from upstairs and I stood up. 'Come on,' the man said to the chef and tried to hoist him up by his armpits.

'All right, all right—I'll go,' the chef said, and he rose, swaying like a sea snake.

I put my shoulder under one of his armpits, the man from upstairs put his shoulder under the other, and we started pushing him back through the kitchen into the sunroom. Anna followed. When we got into the hallway the chef turned around quickly, dislodging his armpits from where they rested on our shoulders, and pinned Anna against the wall. 'You want me, but you can't have me,' he said.

'You're disgusting—fuck off,' she said, shoving his chest with her palms.

The man from upstairs grabbed the chef again and hustled him down the hall into the sunroom. Anna and I stayed in the kitchen.

A few minutes later the man returned. 'He's passed out.' We thanked him and he left.

Anna turned to me: 'That was fucked. That chef has fucking got it coming.'

The next afternoon I held the chef's bottle of Jack Daniel's while Anna spooned toilet water into it. She spooned in as much as she could before it became so diluted the colour changed. 'He won't notice,' she said.

Later in the evening the chef came into the living room, where we were both sitting, with the bottle in his hand. 'How's it going—all right?' he said and took a swig.

'Okay,' Anna said, without turning.

Maybe because Anna came when everything seemed to be out of control, maybe because when I was with her she made me laugh so hard I had to sit on the ground to stop from pissing myself, or maybe because we vanquished the chef together, she stayed with me in the dark flat until the lease was up.

7
FISH

Anna, two small punks and I moved into a five-bedroom house in West Melbourne at the beginning of 2006. There was a spare room for Xochi for when she returned from Canada.

The men who ran the pub up the road owned our house. They had renovated it with some punters before we moved in. When I signed up at the video store the man behind the counter looked at my address and asked, 'What do you think of your paint job?'

'It's fine. It's nice,' I said.

'It's shithouse,' he said. 'I did it. I painted all the windows shut.'

The house was a storm. It heaved and tossed with oversized

personalities. It sucked up extras and spat them out in communal spaces. In the mornings I picked my way through punks and skinheads asleep on the living-room carpet, which was changing colour from beige to charcoal. Funnels of joy, anger, hilarity, irritation, sadness, fatigue and manic excitement whipped up quickly and subsided slowly.

Anna floated through it all, and I clung to her. She made the mundane mythical. Outings with her were electric. Some nights we went to the pub and made up stories about the bottle-shop guy for hours. Other nights she took me backstage to meet bands I'd never heard of and some I had, or we filched art from bar walls for our house, or danced like idiots. She came home in a fire truck once, and another time she arrived clasping metal plaques painted with numbers from the service station up the road. In the late mornings, if we managed to shift from our beds into the kitchen, Anna would retell the night's outing, leaving out the boring bits and exaggerating the exciting parts. I loved these stories almost as much as the outings.

Everyone we knew was from somewhere else and discoveries were shared like swap cards—an abandoned schoolroom up four storeys in Chinatown, still with little chairs and desks; the punk squat in an empty funeral parlour on Sydney Road in Brunswick; the manhole that led to the roof of a Hungry Jack's in the city; a tiny tearoom with sweet, decrepit caretakers; coffee shops filled only with elderly men; pools to break into at night; dive bars; back entrances to pubs.

I didn't think about alcohol, the way I didn't think about eating or breathing. It was just an essential part of existence.

Drugs were big colours—hard ink blots on otherwise pastel routines—while alcohol was everyday.

I drank more than ever. On rare nights I could remember getting home but usually I had no idea what had happened past midnight. I shed personal objects—cards, wallets and phones. I spent Saturdays and Sundays vomiting bile into a saucepan. I started to feel darkness when I drank: a gasping, anxious slide from euphoria into deep nervous anger. It started with small tendrils of anxiety, then my breath became shallow and I started kicking as hard as I could to stay afloat. I drank more to stave off the fall but it was inevitable, and drinking more just made me black out.

I became afraid of what I might say or do when drinking. I took on an early morning Sunday shift as a disability-support worker, thinking that if I had to be somewhere at 8 a.m. it would force me not to drink the night before. It didn't work. Every Sunday morning for six months I scraped myself out from under the covers and half jogged to the train station in the rain, wind or struggling sunshine, stuffing my fingers into my armpits to warm them up, trying to unpeel my eyelids and rubbing my temples to keep them from collapsing into my skull.

Xochi came home from Canada and moved into the front room. I had missed her fiercely and was overjoyed when she got back, but she was unhappy in the house.

Xochi had a reservoir of compassion that I pissed in repeatedly and never managed to taint. She was doggedly patient and shared everything with me—her family, bed, socks, clothes, make-up, and underpants when I'd forgotten to wash mine.

I went to her if I was homesick, frightened or sad. One night I ate four slices of hash cake, fell asleep, then woke up at 1 a.m. convinced I was dying. I went downstairs to Xochi's room and tried to be calm. 'Call an ambulance—I'm dying,' I said.

'You're not dying, you're stoned—drink some juice,' she said, then got up and sat with me in the front doorway of our house. A car passed and we laughed until we couldn't breathe. We sat until the hysteria had passed, then I projectile vomited chocolate cake and she laughed.

When I thought of Xochi I couldn't see where I ended and she began. We were distinct but melted into one another, like the two-tone icing swirl on a marble cake. My love for her overrode jealousy, envy, anger. She was, and is, beautiful, with a fierce face, high cheekbones, blue eyes, black lashes and auburn hair. I couldn't bear to share her and I was envious of the attention she received from men. I was daunted by her sense of purpose.

She became mired in sadness that I tried to help shake and eventually resented. Instead of talking to her I saved up everything I was thinking and yelled at her in bitter, drunken tirades I couldn't remember and she wouldn't repeat. One morning we lay in her bed and I sheepishly apologised for what I couldn't remember saying or doing the night before. I said sorry until I was sick, and sick of myself.

I was terrified that she would stop wanting to be my friend, and yet I acted to ensure that she did. On a warm afternoon in a park by the bay, she had poured a glass of cheap white wine into a plastic cup and said she could never be the friend of someone who slept with anyone she dated. Soon after, she went to Canada and I fucked the artist following a night on cheap beer and weak pills. We used a bright-blue condom someone had left behind. Afterwards I couldn't understand why I'd done it. I decided not to tell her.

Two years later she left the house in West Melbourne, and an angry, volatile relationship with a man she loved, to live in Colombia. 'Look after Nigel,' she said. And I did, in much the same way as I had the artist. We went to a punk picnic, drank half a bottle of whisky each and ended up naked in my bed.

I was a greedy, grasping drunk. I did what I wanted and took what I wanted, and in the aftermath I blamed it on alcohol.

On the loneliest morning I sat in a moving van next to a stranger with a fishbowl on my lap and everything else I owned, which wasn't much—a plywood dresser covered in cracked veneer, an old mattress, a broken armchair I'd found on the pavement and a few green bags of clothes—in the back.

Anna, her boyfriend and I had been living together in Brunswick for a few months. Our friendship, which I had thought impermeable, had grown sore and red, then popped. I resented sharing Anna with her boyfriend and she was tired of my anger. The night it became clear we couldn't live with one another anymore I had got blackout drunk and yelled at her. The next day I couldn't remember what I'd said and she wouldn't tell me, because I was vomiting so much she had to call a doctor, but it was evident something had broken in her because she was more apathetic than concerned.

I looked down. Water from the fishbowl was slopping onto my legs and the car seat. The man I had hired to drive my belongings to the new house became agitated. He pulled into a service station and I ran inside to get a plastic bag.

When the goldfish had arrived there had been two other fish with it—a black fish with bobble eyes and a brown fish with a triangular dorsal fin. We found the brown fish floating at the top of the water, dead, three days later. In the weeks that followed, the goldfish was attentive to the black fish. It rubbed its mouth against her side and we thought it was kissing her. The black fish floated to the top quarter of the bowl and every time she tried to descend the goldfish kissed her. Only the fish was not kissing her: it was biting through her gills. The black fish drowned after hours of trying to suck air through her mouth while the goldfish chewed on her fins and tail.

I didn't like the goldfish very much and it didn't like anyone, but we were all we had, and in hindsight maybe we were similar. We attacked those around us, and then we were alone.

8

ROUEN YOUR LIFE ROAD

Alexander moved out of home when he was eighteen. I had been in Melbourne for two years by then, and Patrick was living in London. The share house Alexander moved into was on Rouen Road, Milton—its inhabitants called it Rouen Your Life Road—and he moved in last, so he got a room that was more like a thoroughfare.

There were four boys living there in all. Two were Alexander's closest friends from school—Toddy, a tall, solid boy with straw-coloured hair; and Matt, thin, with brown curly hair and big eyes.

When I first met Toddy he was so shy that he sat quietly in the corner while we ate dinner, declining my mother's invitations to join us. He was always the first person awake after parties at our house, and while the rest of us slept he silently cleaned the backyard, chucking empties into the wheelie bin, picking plates out of the garden and taking glasses down to the kitchen. We called him Hardworking Todd.

Matt—Dicko to his mates—was drafted into the AFL when he was seventeen. He dropped out and started his own clothing line, which was stocked by a well-known street-clothing store. A few years later he got sick of that and started music production. When I saw him last he had just been in India meditating for four months. He was selling watches he'd designed—the watch face didn't tell the time; it said 'now'—and living in Melbourne, writing about the link between mindfulness and creativity.

I didn't know the third boy so well, other than that his name was Alex, too. He went to school with them.

Rouen Road was the archetypal first share house—chaotic and unsustainable but ridiculous, funny, and without rules. Alexander told me once that if you stayed in the shower for longer than two minutes you became filthier than you had been when you got in. When the inhabitants ran out of toilet paper they had a competition to see how long they could last without it. First they used newspaper, damp from shower puddles. Later, because no one wanted to buy more newspaper, they used glossy magazines.

The house was furnished with couches found on roadside pick-ups. When there was no room left inside the couches were stockpiled in the backyard. By the end of the lease there were thirteen on the lawn among smashed bottles and cartons.

Toddy had a job at an ice works, and he was the only person at Rouen Road who regularly bought food. Both Alexanders stayed on the couch all day watching TV and eating whatever Toddy had stockpiled in the fridge. Dicko lay in bed with his girlfriend, smoking, ashing between the sheets, then stubbing his butts in an empty stubby cooler. The butts burnt holes in the cooler and the cigarettes fell through into a pile on the floor.

I talked to Toddy about Alexander on my back verandah one afternoon a couple of years ago. I ate all the biscuits I had baked for him, and he carefully rolled neat cigarettes while answering my questions. His responses were measured and thoughtful.

Toddy told me they would start their drinking week on Thursday night after football training. One of the pubs in town sold fifty-cent pots and they would compete to see who could spend the least amount of money.

'One night [my mate] Tal went out with like ten dollars and he came back with more money then he went out with, 'cause people used to just drop coins at the bar and you'd pick them up. It was crazy,' Toddy said.

On Friday night they would drink at home, and then on Saturday they would play football. As soon as they had finished football, they would start drinking again. On Saturday night they went out and on Sunday they would wake up hungover and someone would say, 'Let's just go get a carton.'

'You would think, Oh God,' Toddy said, 'but we would do it again Sunday. Then Monday…nothing, Tuesday nothing, Wednesday night you'd have a few and then it'd be Thursday again. Let's start again.'

It was around this time that Alexander started to disappear. There were occasions where everyone from Rouen Road would go out and in the morning they'd ask Alexander, 'What happened to you last night?' and he wouldn't remember a thing.

'There was one particular night where we all went out, and we all came home at different times—you know how you go out together but no one ever comes home at the same time? And we all got home, and we were like, Where was Muir last night? No one knew.

'And everyone's like, Oh, he'll show up. Then he walked into the house hungover as. Shoes in his hand, jeans on, shirt all scraggedy. And we said, What happened to you? And he was like, Oh, I got woken up—I was in the back of a car. He'd got into someone's car and slept in the backseat.'

The car was in an elderly couple's garage. They had come out in the morning to go somewhere and spotted Alexander. They woke him up and the man asked: 'What are you doing, mate?' Alexander rolled over and said, 'I'm sleeping!' then turned around and settled back down. The couple woke him again. He looked up at them, said, 'Oh shit, sorry,' then got up and walked away.

Toddy told me that when Alexander walked out of the garage he was still drunk. He came upon an open house, walked in and sat on the couch for an hour. 'And we're like, Really, why? And he goes, I was so hungover. I just wanted to sit down.'

'You can't do that, man,' Toddy said to him.

Alexander often slept in strange places. 'We'd both be the same,' Toddy said. 'You'd go out and you'd drink until you couldn't drink anymore and then you'd go to get in a cab, you wouldn't be able to get one, and you'd be that tired you'd just find the best place you could.'

'Why did you guys start drinking like that—that much?' I asked.

'I think me and him were probably the worst two at it. Ever since I can remember it's the same thing—you'd drink until you couldn't drink anymore and then you wouldn't know what was going on, so you'd fall asleep somewhere.

'But, yeah, he knew that he was a bad drinker. Not bad—he wasn't violent or anything like that—but he just couldn't remember anything. He'd black out and he couldn't remember a thing. And then he started drinking Golds, mid-strengths, and it was okay. So we'd tell him, Muir, you're drinking Golds today. And he'd be like, Yep, yep, I know.

'And some days he wouldn't, and we're like, No—not tonight, don't drink that, you won't remember a thing. And it was crazy. So he knew about it—he knew when he drank he would just black out and wouldn't remember a thing.'

I spoke to another friend of Alexander's, Kieran. They were studying engineering together. He said one night they'd been partying, and Alexander returned drunk and covered in soot.

'He'd crawled into that burnt-down rollerskating place. He would have known that the floorboards had no structural integrity. But he went up in there by himself and he fell through the floor. And when he came back to ours he was covered in black soot and everyone was wondering where he'd been.'

'He went in there by himself?' I said.

'Well, that's what he was like. He made himself pretty obvious at parties when he drank, he was always happy to talk to anyone and quite a loud character. But he sort of got to the point where his personality became invincible and he started doing weird stuff. Like, for example, he walked along the top of the bridge piers on the William Jolly Bridge. One day he and some other friends were walking along the bridge and he climbed up on the top and walked along the top of the bridge arches.'

The William Jolly is a car bridge connecting the Performing Arts Precinct to the city. Its arches curl above the road like the curves of a Chinese dragon. At their highest point they're nine or ten metres tall.

'He always tested the limits. I've got other mates like that and I've got a cousin exactly like that, but whether he pushes the limits as far as Alex seemed to do is another story. And I think that was a component of his personality amplified by alcohol and having fun,' Kieran said.

'I remember those things not because I was worried about him but because they were the funny stories he had. Like breaking into his ex-girlfriend's house and her parents calling the cops. You would only hear those stories from Muir. And he was always happy to tell people. He was never embarrassed.'

A few years after he finished school, Alexander had enrolled in engineering. He was obviously intelligent, but he'd never really tried hard at anything before. This was different. Complicated sums made sense to him. He didn't know why, he told me, but problems that better students found difficult just seemed to click into place for him. He didn't particularly like it—he just found it easy.

The only thing he liked about engineering was that he would

get to travel. One night we were speaking on the phone and he told me it was all he wanted to do. 'I'll never stop,' he said.

The last time I saw Alexander was in 2009. We were in Adelaide for our grandfather's funeral. There were hundreds of people there, and the wake, which started at twelve in the afternoon and finished sometime the next morning, was big and boozy.

Mum and Dad went back to the hotel at 10 p.m. but Alexander and I stayed on, weaving between aunts, uncles, distant cousins, family friends, people who'd known us when we were small but whom we hadn't seen in years.

At around 1 a.m. I realised I hadn't seen Alexander for a while. I walked around asking people if they knew where he was, but no one else had seen him for at least half an hour. I took a cab back to the hotel to see if he'd gone home, but he wasn't there. I didn't know what to do, so I walked onto the street and called the police. 'Where are you?' asked the operator.

'I don't know,' I slurred. 'I don't know—Adelaide, I think? My brother's gone missing.'

'Where were you?' she said.

'My grandfather's funeral, my aunt's house. I don't know where it is.'

'We can't help you if you don't know where you are and you don't know where you were.'

'But he's missing.'

'What does he look like?'

'He's tall, with hair and a suit. He's young. About twenty.'

'Okay,' the operator said. 'Leave us your number and if

anyone fitting that description is found we'll call you. That's the best we can do.'

'Fine—I'll find him myself,' I said.

I hailed a cab and slid into the front seat. I was largely incoherent but I managed to babble to the driver that I wanted to go to the area where my aunt lived and drive the surrounding streets to see if I could find my brother.

'Where is that?' the driver asked.

'Norwood. It's in Norwood,' I said, exasperated, then fell asleep.

The driver shook me awake when we got to Norwood, and we drove down a few streets. 'Is this okay—is this what you wanted me to do?' the driver asked.

'Yes,' I said. 'Keep driving.' But I was struggling to keep my eyes open and after we'd been down three or four streets without success I said, 'He's not here. Could you please take me back to the hotel.'

When I woke the next morning my brother was asleep in the other bed. 'Alexander,' I said. 'Alexander. Wake up.' He opened his eyes. 'Where were you last night? I was really worried. I called the police. I tried to come and find you.'

'I don't know,' Alexander said.

'Really?'

'Yeah. I think I was in the hills. I was about forty minutes from here, anyway.'

'But the wake was only ten minutes from here. How did you get there?'

'I can't remember.'

'How did you get home?'

'I can't really remember, hey.'

'You're crazy. How could you not remember?'

'I don't know! I just can't remember.'

I wonder now why I didn't say anything. Why it didn't occur to me to tell him: 'You drink too much, and you really can't drink. It's not funny when you disappear. Anything could have happened to you.'

But I know the answer. I didn't say anything, because I also would have had to say: 'I tried to find you, but we could have driven past you three times, for all I know, because I was passing out in the cab.'

And anyway, it was kind of funny that he had gone all the way to the hills.

9

THE LAST MORNING

The last morning I ran around the oval near my house in Melbourne was the morning my aunt knocked on the door at 7 a.m. I was wearing black Dunlop Volleys and mismatched socks. There was a hole in the Volleys where the little toe had rubbed through the canvas. The shoelaces had snapped and been retied a few times, and the shoes were too loose—they were shit—but it didn't matter. I could never run more than a few laps.

It was the last morning for many things, but I didn't know that when I heard the knock. Our friends all used the back gate and no one visited early. I was worried it was the sad, mute girl from next door who sometimes came over to ask for a cup of tea, then sat staring at the floor, so when I opened the door and saw my aunt I was surprised, and relieved. 'Helen! It's so good to see you.'

She shook her head. 'Not good,' she said, and started crying. 'You have to go home.'

It was 13 November 2009. In the early morning of the previous day a policeman had found Alexander's wallet, phone, T-shirt and thongs on the pedestrian walkway of the Story Bridge in Brisbane. No one had seen him since.

The Story Bridge is a cantilever car bridge that spans the Brisbane River, joining Kangaroo Point to the Fortitude Valley cliffs. There's a pedestrian walkway on each outer side. At its highest point the distance from the underside of the road to the river is roughly thirty metres.

When my brothers and I were young, an uncle told us that the bridge could tell stories—that was how it got its name. Each time he drove us across, a voice whispered nonsense tales. Although we never heard the voice in anyone else's car, my uncle denied he was its source.

It was an enchanted bridge then and, even when we were old enough to realise we had been fooled, somehow its enchantment stuck.

Unlike the other city bridges—low, practical and urban—that span the river, the Story Bridge is omnipresent. It threads through the background of the inner city, stitching streets to parks to hotels to office buildings. At dusk thousands of coloured bulbs light its steel valleys and peaks, and small caravans of tourists clamber up the rollercoaster arches to watch the sunset.

Viewed from underneath the bridge is enormous, solid and

comfortingly indestructible—immune to the river's moods. The only indications of a sinister element are the emergency phones and helpline signs along the pedestrian walkway: 'Who cares about you? *We do.* Call Lifeline.' The Story Bridge is an infamous suicide spot.

Alexander disappeared on the last day of his exams for the year. He'd been studying for weeks. After the exam he went to the university bar with his friend Kieran and some other students from the engineering class. Kieran stayed until 9.30 p.m. He told me that he'd asked Alexander if he wanted a lift home but Alexander wanted to stay on. He had money that day, Kieran explained, which was unusual.

Kieran offered to take Alexander's bag. Alexander accepted and told Kieran he'd pick it up from his house the next day, then give Kieran a lift wherever he wanted. The people Alexander stayed with at the bar weren't close friends, more acquaintances, but they were good people, Kieran said.

At some point the group got on the shuttle bus and went into the city, to a rabbit warren of a nightclub beneath a backpacker hotel. At the door a fat bouncer with an earpiece scans proof-of-age cards and driver licences.

Inside the nightclub are two bars. The first overlooks the street. The second is down a sloping ramp in the bowels of the building. Along one side of this bar is a row of dark booths. Against an entrance pillar muscular men with gelled hair play a coin-operated punching-bag game while bartenders in tight fluoro singlets serve vodka mixed with Mother Energy drink. On pole-dancing platforms backpackers gyrate to infectious pop.

My friends and I used to go there during our university years to get drunk cheaply.

The group stayed at the nightclub until sometime after midnight. On their way out one of the boys asked Alexander where he lived and if he'd be okay to get home. He replied that he'd catch a cab to my parents' house, that he'd be fine. Only he didn't go home. He went to the Story Bridge.

That Alexander's personal items were on the bridge was worrying but potentially explicable. After all, it wasn't the first early morning call my parents had received concerning my brother. Maybe he'd partially undressed to amuse a girl. Or he was in a park somewhere, asleep in the mud under the mangroves.

The cops phoned my parents soon after they found Alexander's gear, and they drove to the Fortitude Valley Police Station.

Two police officers accompanied my parents to the places Alexander sometimes stayed—a share house across the creek, his ex-girlfriend's verandah. They knocked on doors and woke up bleary-eyed friends.

When they had exhausted every possibility, Alexander's case was assigned to two other officers, and Mum and Dad came home.

Patrick had come home from London that year. He was living with my parents and working in construction. At 4.30 a.m., an hour or so after my parents left the station, he went to work. On his way out of the house he saw the police card on the kitchen bench, picked it up and took it with him.

He told me he thought Alexander had been arrested and had absentmindedly, drunkenly, left the card out. He said he didn't want Mum and Dad to find out, in case they went berserk.

During the day Toddy called him. 'Have you seen your brother?' Toddy asked. Patrick said he hadn't but that he'd found the card on the bench.

'He didn't go home last night,' Toddy said.

Patrick didn't think too much of it.

That afternoon, when he walked in after work, Mum was sitting at the kitchen table. 'Where's Alexander?' he asked.

'I was hoping you knew,' Mum replied. 'They found his wallet, phone, shirt and thongs on the Story Bridge.'

He told me later that at that moment he knew Alexander wasn't coming home. 'I knew, I knew that he had either died or been severely injured. From that exact moment there was never any doubt in my mind.'

'How did you know?' I asked him.

'Why would his wallet, phone, shirt and thongs be in a pile on the bridge? After he'd been missing one day, I thought: This isn't him. After two: Case closed.'

In Melbourne, Helen told me I should pack. I pulled a dress and a scarf from an overflowing basket. I couldn't find any clean undies or bras, so I just stuffed the two garments and some toiletries into an oversized bag.

I knocked on my housemate's door. 'My brother's missing,' I said. 'It's probably fine, he's probably just with some girl, but I've got to go home.' For some reason it was important to me that she didn't panic, that I didn't panic. If we didn't panic, it would be okay.

Helsy bought two tickets at the airport and we sat in a café overlooking the runway, drinking expensive cappuccinos and making up scenarios in which Alexander returned home unscathed. On the plane we did the easy crossword and filled in every blank space. It took us the whole trip.

We arrived at my parents' house in the late morning. Patrick met us at the top of the stairs. 'I'm so glad you're here, El,' he said. When he was little, Patrick had tried to follow me everywhere, and I had desperately attempted to lose him, until one day he just stopped trying, and then I was sad. We had always fought a lot, we were very different, but when he met me at the top of the stairs there was no one I was gladder to see. He grabbed me and crushed me tight, and momentarily I felt safe.

The living room was swarming with cousins, aunties, uncles and friends. Everyone was trying to touch me, hug me. I felt crushed by their shock, by the force of their fear. People were speculating about what had happened, crying, comforting, silent, busy, sitting, standing, walking, tending babies, hushing kids, handing out food, phoning husbands and wives, trying to keep out of the way, getting in the way.

About twelve of Alexander's friends were lined up around the pool. Some of them had their legs in the water; some were lying on the tiles. Occasionally one would drag on a cigarette but otherwise their slumped bodies were motionless. They stared into the middle distance, intently examining something invisible to me.

When I fish my mind for memories of that time, those that surface are sharp—my uncle cringing as I ground the gears of the four-wheel-drive; the untimely arrival of two pet parrots my mother had promised in September to mind; Patrick's girlfriend's gift of clothes to wear and five cotton undies in a plastic packet; and the people, like gauze, who padded my immediate family, and stopped us from disintegrating.

I made missing-person posters. They featured a photo of Alexander that had been taken the night before—he was standing between two boys I didn't recognise, wearing a pink shirt and laughing. I gave little piles of the posters to his friends to tape up around places he might have been—his university, the bridge, town.

Patrick and I went together to Toowong, because we thought he might have gone home with someone who attended the university there. We bought gaffer tape and scissors from the supermarket. We taped the posters to telephone poles along the river walkway, and around the Regatta Hotel. We stuck a few near the CityCat stop in case a ferry commuter had seen him.

When we had finished we bought corn chips from the same cashier. He looked at us strangely. 'He thinks we've bound someone up with gaffer tape and murdered them with the scissors, and now we need a snack,' I said to Patrick. It was a dumb joke, but we both laughed hysterically.

A few years later Paddy said that he helped for my sake, but he thought it was pointless. I think maybe I knew it, too. In some way the posters suited my need for drama. I wanted people to know that this person had disappeared—that their lives might still be the same as they were yesterday, but other lives were not. I justified the action to myself by claiming it was important to do everything we could. I thought that, if we gave up, we would have to acknowledge that something really bad had happened.

That afternoon we sat on the back verandah and talked about birds we liked. My aunty described a bird she had seen but didn't know the name of and my father fetched *What Bird Is That?* The discussion moved on, but Dad kept flicking through the pages. Eventually he interrupted: 'Is this it?' He held up the book. 'Yes—that's the one,' my aunty said. Dad started talking about that bird, then other birds, with intensity, occasionally illustrating his point with an image. It was a ridiculous conversation, but strangely comforting, and I found myself pulled into it.

The phone rang and Mum went inside to answer it. She was gone for a while. When she came back Dad asked her who had called. 'It was someone who saw the poster. He said there was a boy in a pink shirt walking across the bridge last night, and he slowed down because he thought it was one of his friends. He said the boy was kind of stumbling and didn't look like he knew where he was going. He drove off when he realised he didn't know him. He thinks it must have been Alexander.'

No one said much.

Mum lay in my bed that night. I can't remember what we talked about. Because we were still pretending for each other, we might have discussed when Alexander would turn up. Maybe we just lay there for a while listening to the loose ceiling fan buzz.

Early the following morning the phone rang while we were eating breakfast. This time Dad answered. He covered the receiver: 'It's Jeff Humphreys—he saw the poster,' he said.

Jeff is an old friend of my parents. Dad was on the phone with him for a long time. He didn't say too much but his murmurs suggested the news was not good.

When he finally hung up we mobbed him. 'What happened? What's happening?'

'Jeff was out running near the Botanical Gardens. He's still there now. He can see something in the river. He thinks it's a body.'

Patrick's girlfriend called while Dad was talking. Patrick answered the phone, and I heard him ask her to repeat what she was saying. He sounded agitated. When he got off the phone he was ashen. 'Tonya's crying. She says all the river traffic's stopped. She's on a ferry near QUT. There's a police boat fishing something out of the water.'

We waited.

The officers who were working on the case arrived about an hour and a half later. We all sat in our living room, the police on one couch and the rest of us arranged in a semicircle around them.

The officers were serious and slightly nervous. We were all very nervous. As if in the final seconds of a flagging football match we held each other's hands, clasped shoulders, rubbed backs, leaned forward in fearful expectation. Everyone knew what the outcome would be but even then, crazily, I think we were still hoping for a miracle play.

'Earlier this morning we pulled a body out of the river,' the male police officer said. 'Its fingerprints match the ones we have on file for Alexander. I'm so sorry.'

Paddy stood up, walked into the corner, covered his face with his hands and started to rock. From his mouth came the sound of a kettle boiling. It was the strangest sound I'd heard a human make, and it cut through the other sounds for a long time. Even now when I think of it, I get chills. Someone told me later he was keening.

I went into the bathroom and retched over the toilet. I couldn't vomit, although I badly wanted to.

Mum came in a few minutes later. 'Are you okay?' she asked.

'Yep—are you?'

'I feel like something's been drained out of me,' she said.

I don't know what people did in the few hours after the police left. Although I was never a tidy person, it seemed important just then that everything was orderly, so I rearranged items on a shelf in the back room for a while.

After I'd tired of the shelf, I went into the backyard and lay down under the mango tree. It was the only place I could find without people. I thought about how lonely it must have been to die in the river.

My oldest friend, a girl who lived across the street from us when we were growing up, came and sat next to me a little later. We didn't talk much, but we must have been there for ages, because when I got up my thighs were blistered with green-ant bites.

That afternoon the backyard filled with friends, relatives and neighbours. There were at least a hundred people, many of whom I hadn't seen for years. My parents had organised for a priest to say Mass.

It was the type of afternoon I've only experienced in Brisbane at the end of the year, when the midday heat and glare that presses the sky into the earth has passed, and slowly, slowly it comes to be that the air is purple, the grass is cold, the crickets are calling with their legs, and the scent from a tree I've never known the name of makes you catch your breath and wonder that you're living. It's a magical time—and that afternoon was a magical afternoon of sorts, because it was the first afternoon in a dislocated world, one in which Alexander didn't exist.

Then and afterwards, I watched my mother with wonder and worry. She seemed to have become an automaton. Over the next few days she hugged weeping friends and relatives; received condolences; organised funeral notices, Mass booklets, priests, coffin handles, bouquets and the wake.

My dad cried and cried, yet at least he was there: I knew he was still alive. It was like Mum had swallowed lye, but instead of searing her flesh it had run through her body and cauterised her emotions. It bemused her, too. She kept saying, 'I think I'll probably collapse sometime—but right now I feel fine. I feel nothing.'

The following evening we went to sit with the coffin. The funeral home was an old house in Bowen Hills. We were greeted by one of the attendants, a young, thin, whispering man, overly attentive and almost comically grave. His neat hair was parted to one side and he bowed slightly at intervals.

He took us into a long room filled with rows of chairs. The coffin was at the front; behind it was a floral arrangement. It was quiet except for piped music. We sat.

It felt stupid to sit beside a plywood casket with gilt handles and a plastic silver-coloured crucifix. All the edges of death had been smoothed over by the music and huge floral arrangement, the ugly carpet and soft lighting.

The funeral directors said it would be best not to look at the body, so the casket was closed. Dad lifted up one end of the coffin to make sure Alexander was in there. It was heavy, so I guess he was.

Alexander had been in the river three days by the time they found him.

When a corpse is in a body of water at first it sinks to the waterbed. In a river it drifts with the tides, nudging car bodies, trolleys, branches, boat carcasses, building materials, sunken jetties and pylons. The skin goes very soft and white. The soles of the feet and the palms wrinkle like when you're in a bath too long, only much worse. If there are fish or crustaceans in the water, they nibble at the flesh: first they eat the lips and nose.

After a few days the decomposing body fills with gas and floats face down to the surface, the arms acting as ballast. If the body has dragged on the bottom it becomes blackened and bruised. And the eyes bulge.

That is why they wouldn't open the coffin lid.

I don't know whether Alexander went to the Story Bridge by cab or on foot. But, when he arrived there, he made his way to the middle. He took off his shirt and thongs, and pulled his wallet and phone out of his pockets. Then he climbed over the waist-high railings and jumped.

It takes approximately two and a half seconds to fall thirty metres. I often wonder what—if—Alexander thought during that time. Did he sober up in the tepid November air long enough to curse in fear, or did he enjoy the brief feeling of the wind's thin resistance pushing his hair and arms towards the sky? Did he watch the streetlights above the cliff blur yellow, then disappear, as the river's skin ruptured under his weight and he sank?

For some years I didn't know exactly how he died. My parents' propensity to protect us meant that when the coroner's report arrived my mother didn't discuss it with us. Or maybe it slipped her mind, as things did during that time. I think perhaps it was enough for her to wake each day, get out of bed and try to control her anger.

In 2013 I ordered a copy of the coroner's report for myself. It arrived in an innocuous white business envelope. When I read it I discovered that Alexander had drowned. It wasn't his flight that was flawed—there was no extreme angle to his fall. He made it into the water intact.

I thought at least he'd broken a bone, perhaps cracked his neck or split his legs. I thought there must have been a reason he couldn't get to the surface again, that his damaged body became an anchor and pulled him down—but he drowned.

He was a strong swimmer. He should have floated to the surface and set out for the bank. Perhaps the shock of the impact caused him to draw breath too soon, or he choked on spray. Perhaps, disoriented, he swam towards the riverbed, opening his mouth for oxygen and gulping dirty water instead.

Was there a knifepoint of consciousness or lucidity that, however briefly, sliced through the alcohol haze? What did he think about then? Did he remember us—Mum, Dad, Patrick, Gran and me? Was he sad or scared? Did he know he would die? Was he filled with wonderment at his own audacity?

Alexander had a blood-alcohol level of 0.238, just under five times the legal limit for driving. No other drugs were detected in his system.

With that much alcohol in your body you're likely to display some of the following physical symptoms: loss of understanding, impaired sensations, memory blackout, disorientation, mental confusion, dizziness, exaggerated emotional state, increased muscular incoordination, staggering gait, slurred speech, vomiting, incontinence and an increased pain threshold. It's possible you'll fall unconscious. Drink a little more, push your level to 0.35, and you're at the lower end of the bracket that could lead to overdose and death.

Alexander weighed about eighty-five kilograms. To reach a level of 0.238 he would have had to drink ten pints of beer. It is likely he was displaying at least some of the above behavioural signifiers of drunkenness. Certainly the person who rang about seeing him on the bridge said that he was. Ideally, much earlier, he should have been cut off by staff at the venues he visited.

His birthday party would have been held a few weeks later. I had booked my tickets to come up for it, and some of Mum's sisters were coming, too. Alexander couldn't stop talking about it. Toddy told me that Alexander thought it was going to be the best twenty-first all year.

'It was going to be awesome. He was going to invite all our mates that we hadn't caught up with in ages,' Toddy said.

'You know how, when you finish school, everyone just splits up and there are different cliques that you hang out with? Well, me and him used to hang out with heaps of different people all the time. So before his twenty-first he was like, I'm going to invite all those people.

'It wouldn't have been huge,' Toddy said. 'He just wanted it to be sunny. With a slip-and-slide.'

10
WHITE NOISE

I returned to Melbourne. It wasn't as difficult as I thought it might be—just odd. I felt couched in white noise. My friends and acquaintances interacted with me like I was blown glass and they were wearing welding gloves. Their concern was evident, but most people tried not to talk about what had happened. If they did, the subject would be broached tentatively, as if they were afraid to crush me.

It was strange, because I wanted to talk about it compulsively, but I felt like I couldn't find a way past their fear of upsetting me. Please ask me about this thing that has happened, I wanted to say. Please ask me about my brother.

I tried to patch Alexander back together with stories. I asked his friends to write to me about what they remembered of him. The stories were heartfelt and funny but they were all about Alexander getting drunk. Alexander taking his clothes off, sliding through mud; Alexander passing out on the verandah of his ex-girlfriend's house, or pulling a table and chairs into the moshpit at Splendour in the Grass so he could sit and relax in the middle of the maelstrom. I used to love those stories but now when I read them I felt empty. I filed them away.

I dreamt about Alexander most nights. The dreams were similar. I would be playing with Patrick and some of the kids from down the road, and he would try to join in. I would say to him, 'You can't play anymore, Alexander. You're dead,' and wake up feeling awful.

Everything was infused with my brother's nonexistence. Patrick stopped killing insects in case of reincarnation. I stopped having sex with the person I was seeing. 'I can't. What if he's watching?' I said.

The city got hot, like it always did, but the heat tightened and itched like sunburnt skin. The endlessness of the metropolis, its closed concrete embrace, chafed.

At work one day, I was eating a piece of sushi during my lunch break when I found a copper staple in my mouth. I stopped eating and went back to the sushi restaurant with the half-eaten California roll and the staple. I lined up behind the other customers. When I got to the cash register I said, 'I don't want my money back—I just want to show you the staple that was in my sushi.' The girl who was serving got the chef. I held out the roll and the staple. 'Look,' I said. 'There was a staple in my California roll.'

'But we don't have staples in the kitchen or restaurant,' the chef replied.

'You do,' I said louder. 'Here it is.' And I held the copper staple aloft so everyone could see.

'We don't have staples in the kitchen. What do you want?' the chef yelled.

'I want you to admit you had a staple in your sushi. I want you to admit it was in your sushi!' I was screaming now. I wanted to scream at the chef all day. I wanted to take him outside and crack him between the eyes with my fist until his broken brain fell in chunks out of his nose. I wanted him to smack me hard in the mouth until I was spitting teeth, then break each of my fingers. I wanted us to fuck each other up so bad the white noise was gone.

'DO NOT EAT THE SUSHI!' I screamed at the diners. They stared at me, annoyed.

'There are NO STAPLES IN THE KITCHEN!' the chef screamed back, and I walked out and slammed the restaurant door.

I went back to where I worked—a bookshop and stationer, which sold small and medium and large staples of different thicknesses, for different-sized paper stacks, in silver and copper.

My workmate was making a cup of tea at the sink when I came in through the back entrance. 'Never, ever buy sushi from next door,' I said, and tried not to cry.

Upstairs, where I had been eating, were clumps of staples and single staples scattered over the desk and floors. Maybe I'd put my hand down and one had stuck to a finger. Or maybe I'd somehow flicked it onto the plastic sushi tray. I felt ashamed, and it made me angrier.

It was daylight savings and warm, and Melbourne was always beautiful in summer, but I didn't notice. I had a pair of green suede boots that were too hot and pinching. I wore them every day until I walked holes into the soles and the holes let water in and the heat and the water turned my skin to agar and I grew a foot fungus. I went to work, scratched my feet and drank. All I wanted to do was sleep.

A friend tried to distract me by taking me to the art gallery. She thought I might like one of the exhibiting video artists. We sat in a dark room and waited for the video to start. The sound of recorded rain came on and the screen became slightly lighter. A shadowy, human-shaped image appeared far away. It started walking towards the foreground and its features became apparent. The expression on its face was sombre. At some point a gauzy material, or maybe simulated rain, prevented the image from walking any further. It stopped and stared sadly out at the audience. I had a program: I read the work's description in the dull light. 'The images represent souls who are trying to make contact from the afterlife.'

I looked up at my friend. She was staring at me, aghast. 'I'm so, so sorry,' she whispered. 'I had no idea. Do you want to leave?'

'No, it's fine,' I said as another sad human image came into focus, and it was fine because I couldn't feel anything.

Afterwards she apologised again. 'I'm sorry. I'm really sorry. That just made everything worse.'

'It's okay, really. I'm fine,' I said.

'Oh God, and I was running late, too. Did I tell you why I was late?'

'No, why?'

'I went to get money, but someone had shat on the ATM. There was a big shit on the keypad.'

A few days later my friend Laura called. 'Let's go visit your aunt in South Australia,' she said.

'I don't know,' I replied, but Laura could convince me to go anywhere, and fifteen minutes later I had changed my mind.

That was the last summer I lived in Melbourne. I was tired of the things I had once loved about the city. I was tired of walking through its streets. I wanted to get out.

11
WILLIAM CREEK

My mum's eighth sibling, Miriam, took over the lease of the William Creek pub at the beginning of 2009. That year the town's permanent population was three—Mim; her husband, Bruce; and Trevor the pilot.

William Creek is a couple of houses, some dongas, a caravan park, a hangar, a couple of petrol pumps and Australia's first solar-powered phone. There's a space-junk museum in the caravan park: some broken rocket bits on concrete plinths in the dirt. The rockets were launched from Woomera and collected by William Creek's former publicans.

That year it had rained in South Australia and, for the first time in years, Lake Eyre flooded. Instinctively the coastal birds knew, and they flew inland to feed and breed in the saltwater. One of the pilots who was working for Trevor told me that sometimes when he flew over the lake he got confused, because the water was like a mirror and the whole desert looked like sky.

At the end of December, Laura, her housemate, her housemate's best friend and I hired a four-wheel-drive in Adelaide and set off for the pub.

On the first night we stayed with my aunt Helen in her bluestone house under the mountains. It was hot in the sun but grapes were growing along the eaves and under the washing line were wooden buckets overflowing with herbs. We arrived in the late afternoon and picked our way through the spiky grass surrounding her property to the creek bed. In the dirt around an abandoned house on the next property we found some small glass medicine bottles. They were everywhere if you looked, like the railway sleepers and twisted rotting metal and sheep bones.

In the evening my other aunt and some cousins came round and we ate and drank, but not with the furious intensity of the wake; and the air was cool; and my uncle, who looks like Lou Reed and doesn't move his lips much when he speaks, showed us how to dance like a man he'd been in the army with; and it was good to feel like laughing again, and to be with my mum's family, who are warm and funny and flawed and wonderful.

The next day we left for the desert through the Flinders Ranges. The trip is blurry now, most things from around that time are blurry, but I remember the settler line—the broken stone houses that got eaten by the desert because the Europeans were fooled by the grass that looked lush when they arrived yet, once it had been grazed for a season, never grew back. The empty houses litter the area like giant cicada shells—monuments to the hopeless optimism of a people who didn't understand the land.

In the middle of the day we came around a bend. There were two dark crags and, between them, the desert was glazed to the horizon with a thick white salt crust that might have been snow if it weren't so hot—it was the edge of the lake. We stopped the car, got out and walked down to its muddy edge.

It was difficult to breathe in the heat. It was the kind where it feels like you are cold because the sweat evaporates so quickly from your skin. We walked along the mud out to the salt, and our feet sank into its softness, and I became worried, because what if the mud sucked us in and we were petrified like some of the black tree skeletons that stood in relief against the stark white?

Someone had died out there recently—a Swedish tourist whose car got bogged out near the lake. She was with her husband. He stayed to look after the car and she struck out to find help. She died and he lived. 'Don't leave your car,' people everywhere told us. 'If you break down, just stay put. You're more likely to survive.'

By the time we arrived at William Creek, west of Lake Eyre, it was late afternoon. Mim was waiting out the front with her dog. Pig didn't bark much. He sat on the other side of the bar, on people's feet, and leant his whole body up against their legs. Mim said his breed was Tibetan foot dog, and some punters believed her. He was friendly, with tan splotches on his face and back, and Mim was terrified someone would steal him. Her other dog had been bitten by a snake and died when they first arrived.

When we got out of the car, Mim hugged us the same way Mum and all six of her sisters hug, as if they're koalas and you're a branch.

The William Creek Hotel was built in 1887. It's one of the only wooden pubs in Australia in its original condition. There are thousands of business cards, ID cards, driver licences, credit cards, EFTPOS cards, membership cards, passports and beer mats covering the walls, like the scales of a baked fish.

Out the back of the pub are a couple of dongas with rattling brown air-conditioners and floral curtains, and two slightly more luxurious cabin blocks that have bathrooms. We stayed in the dongas and washed in bore water, which covered everything with a fine layer of red dirt, and turned our hair as dry and brittle as the grass we'd walked on at Helen's place.

William Creek was built on the Ghan and the railway sleepers still rot in the red dirt. The train stopped coming in the 1980s and there's no reason the town should still be alive. But the pub is a small, strong heart in the midst of kilometres of emptiness. If you stand in one spot and spin around you can see the horizon in every direction.

I love pubs like these. I love their dark-wood panelling, and the smell of stale beer, and the jukebox, and the stories people tell. A year after our 2009 visit, it's where people will camp out when the track gets flooded for a week. It's where the mail comes. It's where the locals, from thousand-acre desert farms, gather to socialise. Wherever Mim goes she creates and holds together communities—little ecosystems form around her pubs.

We spent the week in William Creek swimming in the lagoon that formed out near the dam because of the rain. We propelled ourselves along on the mud around submerged desert trees filled with cockatoos that came for the desert grasses.

One morning we flew to Coober Pedy to buy dresses from the op-shop for New Year's Eve. The pilot didn't tell us where the sick bags were so we'd try harder to hold off vomiting, and all of us were panting with nausea when we disembarked. We read books and drank beer, ate and slept. In the deep afternoon we went for walks out to the edge of town to inspect the rusty bits of debris, and at night we sat with Mim after she'd finished working and everyone told stories.

On New Year's Eve the pilots dressed up in drag and everyone from the surrounding properties came into town.

We danced until three, then walked out to the dam. It was a full moon, so we didn't need torches, and we floated in the water, looking up at the sky. I slept for an hour, then woke for a sunrise as red and gold as nectarines.

That night, one of the pilots took us out to a dump at the edge of town. It was full of old bottles—medicine, beer, spirits, milk. We hunted for blue glass in the fading light because the pilot told us it was the most valuable. 'People come out here just to look for it,' he said.

When I looked up a blue moon was rising over the desert. I stood to watch, and Laura and the pilot did, too. The rim of the world was pink, pastel purple, then navy; the day had cooled and the flies were gone.

At the edge of night I thought about how, when we were kids, my brothers wouldn't walk up the stairs that led to our bedrooms without me. Our rooms backed onto a long verandah overhanging the backyard. The boys slept in the middle room on clanking hospital beds my dad had bought second-hand. There were Rugby Union posters on the walls, a white Ikea bookshelf in one corner, and outside a small pot of grass Patrick had dug up from the football field down the road. The boys moved the posters to cover the holes they had made fighting.

At night, bats fought in the banana tree outside, and possums made long, croaking, deep-throated growls. Terrified of the nocturnal sounds, we crept into each other's beds, all daytime slights forgotten. Tangled in sweaty limbs, pulling blankets, shoving bodies across the mattress for more space, fighting in whispers and kicks under the sheets, squashed into each other's bodies, we were alive, untouchable, safe.

12
BUENOS AIRES

On a hot day in January 2010 I flew to Buenos Aires. It had always been my intention to live there. I had been saving money for three years and had bought the ticket before Alexander died. After he died I was confused about what to do. I thought perhaps it should be something magnanimous—return to Brisbane to monitor the welfare of my family—but I was not that selfless and the Argentina plan was already in motion.

When I arrived in Buenos Aires it was overcast. It was frequently overcast, and if you stepped on a cracked paver on the old tiled sidewalks your foot went through the ground into a black puddle.

I moved into an apartment with a loft bed in an old house.

There were pot plants on the landings and the owner held expressive-dance classes a few nights a week. In a big room downstairs people in baggy shirts and tights howled, laughed and pounded on the wooden floors until late in the evening, while upstairs rangy cats climbed in and out of the windows and onto the cupboards and into the beds.

The summer air was thick with mosquitoes. Before dawn their violent crescendo became unbearable and I would pull the sheets over my head, frenziedly slapping my hands down around my face and slamming my palms onto the mattress. Every morning my pillowcase was stained with smeared black and red carcases.

Buenos Aires was frightening, beautiful, dirty. I picked my way along the dog-shit-covered footpaths, past stately apartment buildings with crumbling façades; past the graffitied shells of abandoned banks; past another rhythmic picket line; past beggars, businessmen, bookshops, shoe shines, antique stores, key cutters, ice-cream parlours, open manholes, Peruvian restaurants, laundries, grocers, bakers, bird-shit-covered monuments, and small green parks with ornate fences and clowders of feral cats.

There was a rumour about a man with a handgun who lived around the corner from my apartment. He sat all day in his dark front room, like a spider, watching and listening for tourists. When he sighted prey he stepped into the light, brandishing his weapon. The person who told me about him couldn't confirm if the gun was loaded or empty, but the victims handed over their valuables without protest. The man was known to the police but not bothered by them.

The chaos of the city manifested up top—subway strikes, potholed footpaths and picket lines. But underneath, everyone from the beggars to the suits was toiling away industriously at some endeavour. Kids juggled at traffic lights in the morning and afternoon, then with perfect timing canvassed the stopped cars for cash before the lights changed. An elderly lady adorned with religious medals stood in a park near my apartment, pleading for pesos in a singsong cadence. Musicians in tuxedos played violins on street corners. Accordionists jumped on and off the Subte—the subway—deftly swinging through swaying carriages. Pickpockets positioned themselves in clots of commuters at train doors, slipping silent tentacle arms into the open shoulder bags of women who, in the rush to get a seat, temporarily loosened their sarcophagus stance and let their bags swing behind their shoulders.

In some ways it was the perfect place to be after Alexander's death, because things fell apart regularly and unexpectedly. Children disappeared and were never seen again, money suddenly lost its worth, banks shut, streets shut, the Subte shut, roads flooded, slums ripened and shrivelled—and the city thundered on. These regular shocks imbued people with pessimism that forced them to live in the moment, or with dogged fury that spurred them to demand answers from the past: like the Mothers of the Plaza de Mayo, women whose children had been disappeared by the militant Argentine government in the 1970s and '80s. They picketed the pink government house every Thursday, demanding to know what had happened to their children and grandchildren.

At night, if I only had to go a short distance, I trotted quickly, twisting my head from side to side and scanning for danger. If I had to go further I caught a cab. At first, thinking I was being egalitarian, I sat in the front seat, until one night at the end of a trip during which the driver had shifted nervously the entire time, I learnt why I had never seen another lone traveller sitting up front in a taxi. 'Never,' the driver said shaking his head, wagging his left forefinger and patting the front seat with his right hand.

'*Por qué?*'

'*Porque de esos*,' the driver said, and he put his left hand down the side of his seat; then, grasping his left wrist with his right hand, he pretended he was pulling something out. When his left hand emerged his index and middle fingers were pointing forward, his thumb was sticking up in the air, and his pinkie and ring fingers were curled into his palm. He held his hand in the air so that the index and middle fingers pointed at me, then bent his thumb. 'Because of guns, thieves,' he said.

A few years after this night, following two fatal drunken one-punch attacks in Sydney's Kings Cross, the New South Wales government introduced legislation designed to curb excessive drinking and prevent violence in well-fraternised nightspots. Media coverage of alcohol consumption in Australia was extensive. At the time I was back in Brisbane and I had a housemate from Colombia. He remarked to me one night: 'We could never drink like Australians do. Here you go out and you are *borracho, borracho, borracho*. But this is okay because there is no danger, except from other drunks. In Colombia, if we drank like you, we would be dead. Someone sober would mug us. In Colombia, you have to stay alert or else.' He curled his fingers into a gun shape, cocked his thumb and clicked his tongue to mimic the release of a bullet. I recalled the Buenos Aires taxi driver's late-night warning and stopped myself from arguing.

Buenos Aires was the first place I had been where, for reasons of safety, I had to curb a long-established habit of getting drunk and walking the streets. In Melbourne I had trespassed, shouted at diners, stepped onto busy roads with a palm held out to stop the traffic, stolen floral displays, pissed in busy alleyways, and tried to get into hotel rooms by hoping the common surname I pulled from my soupy brain and slurred at the front desk matched the room number I made up. I was an idiot.

There you had to pay attention in cabs and on the streets. Xochi came to visit for a few weeks. As we were coming out of a train station one night we were mugged by a junkie with one arm in her coat and the other moving like a proboscis, with a thick hand on the end. She shoved it deep into my bag looking for cash, pulled out a Chilean note, then thankfully called off her partner who was loping across the street towards us with a hand in his jacket, too.

Maybe there was more drunkenness in Buenos Aires than I knew about, but I never saw it. It wasn't that the *porteños*—the locals—were opposed to psychoactive substances. Cocaine was easy to come by if you were looking for it. But, although the city was open all night, there wasn't the same frenzied street revelry I was used to.

The neat Argentines seemed to note drunken misbehaviour

in public with press-lipped embarrassment or silent approbation. On the Subte one morning I heard a group of young *porteño* women break into accented English. 'Oh my God, I'm so drunk,' one said mockingly. 'I'm like, really, really wasted,' said another, squinting and pretending to sway with intoxication. They all laughed nastily. I shifted uncomfortably in my seat.

On the few occasions I did see a drunk person it was a foreigner or someone from the margins. A drunk with a heavy beard twisted a piece of metal onto my middle finger one night to make a ring. He was one of the artists who lined the streets near the city centre, selling twine bracelets and cheap metal jewellery from blankets that could be packed up easily if the cops came. We shared a swig of warm sweet wine from a bottle he was carrying and he gave me a hard hug goodbye, digging his fingers into my upper arms and pressing his cheek into mine. Later I found that, along with the ring, he had given me nits.

Buenos Aires nightclubs were famous, but I only went to one, once. We got there at midnight and the crowd was still sparse. A friend ordered drinks and we danced for a while, then I had to go to the toilet.

The bathrooms in Buenos Aires usually had attendants. You paid them a peso for toilet paper. In this one the attendant was a girl in her late teens who sat on a stool next to the hand dryer. She was dressed in jeans, a black T-shirt and sneakers, and she had made up her face with black eyeliner and mascara. When I came out of the toilet there was a bread roll on her knee and she was getting a little plastic sandwich packet of ham and cheese out of her backpack. At the sink a couple of well-dressed women chatted in Spanish and spread lipstick over their lips. They were younger than me, about the same age as the bathroom attendant, who looked tired and small and pissed off. She should have been out dancing with her friends, not trying to make dinner on her lap while handing out sheaves of folded toilet paper. I lurched towards the sink and fumbled at the taps feeling unutterably stupid.

I had never thought of drinking as a privilege. I thought of it as inevitable or a right. It was ridiculous, but this was the first time it had dawned on me that you needed money for drinking, not just for the alcohol, but to pay cover charges, find transport and lose a day of work. It didn't occur to me that people might not go out because they couldn't afford to. Even when I had nothing, there was always money to spend in a bar. I went home chastened.

On my first evening in the city I had eaten dinner early at a tourist restaurant. I ordered a wet salad with anaemic tomato slices and tasteless cheese, and the small waiter asked me simple questions in English. 'I finish in one hour,' he said. 'Will you take beer with me?'

'Yes,' I said, because I was lonely.

He took me to a grimy bar opposite a theatre. We ordered thin Argentine beer. I talked in a lumpy Spanish watered down with English words and he spoke in the peculiarly formal, stilted English he'd learnt from textbooks, tourists and Alfred Hitchcock films. We barely understood one another, but it was pleasant enough. He asked me back to his house to see the garden on his roof, and I agreed. On the way I wondered if he might kidnap me, so I stopped speaking and memorised the route.

The waiter's name was Rodrigo, and although he only had three shirts they were always neatly pressed. So were his trousers, which had a crisp centre seam. Rodrigo's father, Hugo, was an ageing heavy-metal singer, unknown except in rural Argentina and the outer suburbs of Buenos Aires. Hugo had prostate cancer and sometimes had to tape a catheter bag to his leg when he performed.

One evening Rodrigo, Rodrigo's cousin, my friend Vibeke and I took the bus through the suburbs to see Hugo's band play. They were headlining—Hugo was the last to appear onstage. An electric fan at the side of the stage blew his long curly hair back. Halfway through the set Hugo ripped his shirt off and his potbelly erupted over the waistband of his leather pants. The maelstrom of black-clad metalheads next to the stage stopped, swung their necks so arcs of sweat droplets formed mohawks in the air, roared, then resumed whirling. Rodrigo stood, completely still, in the shadows near the bar. He wore one of his neat polyester button-down shirts and his hair was combed. There was a half smile on his face.

After the set we went backstage. His father was sitting on the one chair in the room with his knees splayed. A woman in her twenties sat on his thigh. Hugo only briefly acknowledged Rodrigo and ignored the rest of us. It was 6 a.m. If I had still been out in Australia at this time, which I had managed only once or twice in my life, I would not have been able to spell my own name. Here, almost everyone was sober.

Rodrigo's bedroom was on the roof of an old house that had once housed a large family. It was a warren of rooms along verandahs and around a patio where a motley collection of boarders lodged. To get to his room you passed through an old metal security door and climbed up a small stone staircase. The room was bare except for a camp bed, a desk, a microwave with a cooktop and a closet. There was a small round window at one end. 'Like a ship,' he said. Through the window you could see the dome of a Spanish-style church a few blocks away and, next door, the shell of a house and the vine-covered wasteland beyond it. On the roof were garden beds where Rodrigo grew clippings he'd stolen from the botanical gardens, an outdoor shower, and a concrete bench where we sat and drank beer the first night I went home with him.

Rodrigo earned six hundred pesos a month—about 120 Australian dollars—waiting tables. He subsisted on saltines and maté, and bought his few clothes from a woman at the market in the old barrio of San Telmo. When it was cold he wore a Cossack's fur hat and a vintage Hermés scarf he had found on the side of the road. Every object he owned was precious. He once had a complicated scheme of using tokens to steal money from the state, but I didn't understand it too well and his English was too limited to explain it properly.

The night I met him he told me his name meant rich and famous. 'I am rich because there is nothing that I want, and I am famous because my friends and family love me,' he said.

I told him my brother had died, and he said: 'Why do you think about that? That is finished. He is a phantom now.' Rodrigo pronounced phantom with a plump and perfect 'o'. He stared at the sky. 'The clouds look pessimistic tonight.'

I laughed in shock and afterwards, in my apartment, I cried. It was functional crying, like turning on windscreen wipers or a sprinkler. I'd read in a book that the death of a loved one could bring on sudden and unexpected tears. It was true, although the act felt empty. I wasn't sure if I was crying because I had to or because I was acting, trying to emulate normal sadness. I felt dry and wrung out—a skin-covered skeleton ballooning around a formless, roaring void.

13

DEAN

By the end of summer, I was losing air. I started laying plans to leave Buenos Aires. I wanted to make my way down to Patagonia, and I asked Rodrigo if he would come with me for a while if I bought him a bus ticket.

We caught an empty night bus to the provinces one weekend, to a town with a huge lake, midway down the country. Rodrigo had brought his tent and we found a place to camp right on the lake, just outside the town. In the evenings we roasted sweet potatoes on hot coals. I drank plastic mugfuls of wine and Rodrigo sipped maté. Every morning I went swimming in the freezing water. During the day we tramped around the mountain.

Like his city, Rodrigo stormed and stilled quickly. Midway through our trip we left the lakeside town and went further up the mountain to a small village. When we arrived I asked a handsome German man for directions to a campground. Maybe I blushed when I was speaking to him, because as we walked off Rodrigo turned to me and yelled: 'I'm going home!'

'Why?' I said.

'You think that man is pretty. But I do not think he is pretty. You are stupid.'

'I didn't think he was pretty, Rodrigo,' I said, although I did. 'I was just asking for directions.'

'You are stupid. I am leaving.'

'Please, Rodrigo, just come with me to the supermarket to get a few things. Then you can leave if you still want to.'

Feelings I would only have voiced after a few bottles of wine spilled out of him regularly and easily, without the aid of alcohol. And as soon as he'd unburdened his irritation he became happy again. I was used to being taciturn out of politeness or embarrassment, and used to taciturn people. I found his fearless communication alternately amusing and confronting. I couldn't tell if his ease in expressing emotion was a result of his limited English, or if it was his personality, but I think it might have been a common trait among Argentine people.

On our way back from the village we stopped to wait for the bus. A gaucho rode up to the picket fence of a small house across the road. He stopped and called out a name. A short, middle-aged man with grey-flecked hair and a daffy smile walked out and stood in the yard. He and the gaucho began conversing in rapid Spanish. The gaucho got louder and louder, until he screamed out a final, violent string of words. There was silence. Rodrigo started laughing.

'What did he say?' I asked.

'He said to the man: "You laugh at the misfortune of other men."' It was such a beautiful, impassioned phrase, more suited to a daytime movie than an encounter opposite a bus stop on a dirt road. I started laughing, too.

Rodrigo ran out of money after a few weeks and went back to Buenos Aires. I was sad to see him go, but we quickly fell out of regular contact. Months later, when he found out I was travelling through Chile with someone else, he sent me an angry email entitled: *sos tan pelotuda que no me alcanza decirtelo en ingles*. This translates roughly as: you are such an arsehole that I can't say it to you in English. The email finished: *ahogate en la lava*. This means: drown in lava. It was the nastiest correspondence I had ever received.

A few weeks after he told me to drown in lava he sent another email asking how my trip was going, and we were friends again.

Once Rodrigo had gone I made my way down to Torres Del Paine, a national park straddling the border between Chile and Argentina. In a town that stank of petrol—there was an oil refinery on its outskirts—I bought a supermarket tent. It was cheaper to camp than to stay in hostels, and the campgrounds I had been in with Rodrigo were more picturesque. I planned to pitch it first in El Calafate, the next town on my route.

I arrived at midday. Although it was only the start of autumn, it was cold. On the outskirts of town I found a small campground next to a hostel. The manager showed me around. The small, lumpy plots were arranged around dry gullies, and it was dark. 'It's very cold,' said the manager, rubbing her upper arms. 'Why don't you stay in the hostel? It's only five pesos more.' I agreed.

The hostel was full of cyclists and climbers, all of them men. At dinner I went out to the common area with a bag of pasta and some tomatoes but all the stove burners were in use, so I sat and waited. A scruffy older man with a thick Australian accent asked me where I was from.

'I've made extra food if you want some,' he said. I hesitated. 'Go on, there's heaps.'

His name was Dean and over dinner he told me he was travelling to Alaska. He had bought a motorbike with a sidecar in Argentina's southernmost town.

Dean had made his money growing and selling hydroponic weed in the outer suburbs of Melbourne. He also worked as a fitter and turner in a teabag factory. By the time he was twenty-two he owned two houses outright and was on his way to paying off a third. He'd been travelling for five years. The last place he'd been was Africa. He'd hitchhiked down the east side of the continent, then cycled back up the west. In Côte d'Ivoire he was shot in the stomach. There was a long scar next to his bellybutton where the bullet wound had been stitched up. After he was shot he returned to Melbourne to recover, which took ten months. Once he was fixed he flew back to Côte d'Ivoire and started cycling again. He was the toughest, loneliest person I'd ever met.

After dinner he showed me pictures of the Congo. He'd travelled downriver on a flotilla of boats with a bunch of Congolese people who'd nicknamed him Mama Dean and the Express. The Express was a stove he had that heated water quickly; Mama was because he cooked.

'You should come with me on the bike,' he said, when I left to go to bed.

'Thanks, but I've already got plans,' I replied.

A couple of weeks later I ran into Dean in a tiny town at the foothills of the Andes. He was staying in the best room of the cheapest hostel. Its kitchen was filthy and its walls were constructed from strong papier mâché. He invited me out for a drink but I got to the pub late and he wasn't there. I walked down to his hostel and he was in the common area drinking beer out of a large metal cooking pot. There was a sore on his face and he didn't have enough clothes for the weather.

'I was at the pub and you weren't there,' I said. 'I came to find you.'

'Let's go now,' he said.

We went to the pub. He told me his brother had died when he, Dean, was seventeen. Dean found him sitting in his parents' car in the carport with the windows up and the engine revving. A long tube blew the air from the exhaust pipe through the driver's window.

I told him about Alexander. 'He killed himself,' Dean said.

'No, I don't think so. I don't know.'

'Why don't you come with me?' he asked again.

'Okay,' I said.

A few days later we packed up his bike and left. I blew across the top of an empty beer bottle to signal the beginning of the trip. In hindsight this was prophetic: while my relationship with Rodrigo was marked by the absence of alcohol, Dean and I were smashed much of the time we were together.

The day we left it was grey and cold. Behind us were the snow-covered Andes. In front of us was the rocky Patagonian plain and a dirt road.

Both Dean and I were consumed by the past, by what we'd lost. He was angry and I was angry. We fought the entire way up the bottom wedge of the continent. We fought when we stopped to make sandwiches by the side of the road. We fought in guest-houses where we were only given a bucket of water a day. We fought in hotel rooms foggy with Dean's cigarette smoke. We fought on a snow-covered mountain pass while the bike slipped from left to right, crashing into snow bank after snow bank, and I ran behind because Dean made me get out of the sidecar—he was afraid the whole bike might go over the side. We fought over whether or not to go down the mountain: 'If it snows up here, we're fucked,' Dean said.

'Well, let's go down. Let's go the long way.'

'We could get stuck if we keep going.'

'Dean, we *are* stuck. We've been up here an hour and we've only gone twenty metres.'

'Would you be willing to camp up here? Maybe we can make it.'

'I don't know. Yeah, I guess. Whatever.'

'We only have half a cabbage.'

'This is stupid.'

'Ah, fuck it. If I didn't have you I'd do it.'

During the day our arguments were sober, sniping. At night they were messy, drunken, scrappy. My anger was exhilarating and never slaked. It was like dipping a bucket into a deep well, over and over. Dean fought back or he laughed at me. 'You're crazy, girl,' he said, and that made me angrier.

Sometimes when I stopped to think for a moment, and later when my anger had lessened, I was thankful for the way he soaked up my bile; or caught it, slung it back, and allowed me to vomit out more. There was nothing I could say that he couldn't handle. He let me be sad.

It was cold for him on the bike—much colder than it was for me. A screen protected me but he had nothing and was constantly getting sick. We rode through wind, rain and snow, along potholed roads, highways and the tops of ravines.

On the way down the mountain pass Dean dropped his camera on the road. We realised a few hours later and turned back for it. By the time we got back to the bottom of the mountain path, Dean was cold and cranky and driving too fast. He took a corner quickly and we flew off the road into an embankment. I flipped out over the top of the windshield and landed softly in the mud. Dean managed to keep his seat, but the bike's back brakes were broken.

A few days later we rode for four hours in the rain, without back brakes and along a freeway thick with semitrailers, to a garage where we could fix the bike. I don't think it would have mattered to either of us if we'd needed the brakes on the way. Dean had so much time to think, and he was heavy with the weight of his past. His dead brother, his heroin-addicted sister, loves he'd let slip away, small slights from supposed friends—all of them long gone now.

We travelled roads that sloped up through red autumnal forests and suddenly opened out onto sharp snow-capped peaks; we went through a foggy forest where rubbery leaves dripped with condensation and hid unlikely glaciers; past an enormous lake with primeval rock formations rising from its depths—impenetrable islands smashed by swirling white-capped eddies; a multicoloured town too labyrinthine for street maps; a deep afternoon pond, which reflected a mountain kilometres away; and we camped in an apple orchard, next to a glacial river the colour of the sky. The owner of the orchard came striding to meet us with a bloody carving knife in one hand.

'That's a big knife,' Dean said.

'A fox. I kill it,' the man replied.

Each night we drank, but by the end of our trip we were drinking from mid-morning and finishing when we passed out in the evening.

'You could come with me to Colombia,' Dean said during this time.

'I can't.'

'Maybe we can walk across China.'

'I have to go home. I don't have any money left.'

'I'll pay for you.'

'No, Dean. I'm leaving.'

We had a fight the last night we were together. We were in Santiago, Chile. The next day I would catch the bus back to Buenos Aires. From there I would fly home to Brisbane.

The fight was silly. As usual we had been drinking. A couple sitting next to us in a restaurant kissed. We were watching and laughed. The man saw us and gestured for us to follow suit. I refused. When we left Dean yelled at me: 'All you had to do was kiss me—it was a silly thing—it would have made him happy!'

'Well, I didn't feel like kissing you! Why the fuck do we have to do what some man suggests we do?' I yelled back.

'Because sometimes you have to think of other people and what would make them happy, instead of always thinking of yourself!'

The next morning he dropped me off at the bus stop. He wouldn't talk to me, and he didn't kiss me goodbye, but he stood at the bay until the bus left.

I only saw Dean once after that. He came to Brisbane to stay with me for a week. He had made it to Alaska, he told me. When he arrived there it was winter. He camped on someone's property and got pneumonia. He didn't get medical help until he was coughing up blood, and by that time he had cardiomyopathy. He flew back to Melbourne for treatment but couldn't stand to stay in the hospital and left a few weeks before he was supposed to be discharged, without telling the doctors.

'It's bullshit, all that medical shit,' he said. 'It's a conspiracy. It's poison, the crap they put into your body.' He blew smoke from his mouth. I stared, incredulous. 'I'm on holiday,' he said, then grinned.

Not long after that visit he stopped replying to my emails, which was strange for him, as he usually replied within a day or two. I googled his name and found a death notice from

19 February 2014. He had died in a hotel room in Puerto Cortes, Honduras.

I think about Dean most weeks. He forced me to be accountable for my actions, to look properly at myself and to do things I was afraid of. He had a big heart, little sympathy for self-pity, and he was cuttingly honest. He made me brave enough to face the circumstances around Alexander's death, to start asking questions.

Sometimes I think about how, when I dropped him off at the airport at the end of his Brisbane trip, he turned to me and said: 'I wish you'd stayed with me. I wish you'd come up north. I wish you could have seen it. It was warmer and easier travelling. It was beautiful.'

'I couldn't,' I said.

'I know.' And he smiled in the way he had, which made you understand he was sad and wild, free and full of the joy of it.

Afterwards, when he was out of sight, I cried. I felt keenly aware that the morning at the bus stop in Chile had been a fork in my existence—had I not got on the bus my life may have turned out differently—and the feeling ached. But I had to go home.

14
RIVERS OF GROG

For a long time I blamed my parents for Alexander's death. I raked through childhood memories looking for instances of wrong-doing. I tallied birthdays they had missed to attend conferences, the small sips of alcohol we were allowed to have as children on special occasions, the pressure they had put on us to succeed at school, any harsh words they had used, my dad's commitment to work at the expense of a home life, my mum forsaking work for a home life; too many after-school activities, no television, too few punishments, too many punishments; that we owned too much stuff, were left with babysitters, went to the wrong schools; the alcohol collection wasn't locked up, the house was too big, no one listened to us, we talked about football too much, we didn't have to do the dishes, we were spoilt, we were neglected, we had too much freedom or not enough.

I hoarded the memories as fuel for bitter recriminations—the list was exhaustive, hysterical and nonsensical. But if I blamed my parents, it was nothing compared to the blame they piled on themselves.

'I read an article about how important it was for fathers to be at home during a child's formative years,' Dad said at lunch soon after my return from Argentina.

'Oh,' Mum said.

'I should have been at home more,' he said.

'Darling, there's no point thinking about it now. You did what you thought was right at the time.'

On the way to the airport a few weeks after Alexander's funeral Mum had told me she'd been looking after a plant for my grandma, and it died. 'I kill everything,' she said, and started crying. Mum never cried in front of us.

Later on, years later, she said that after Alexander died it took her months before she could remember anything nice she had done for him. During this time she would say things like: 'Remember that time I was talking to the builder and the boys kept annoying me? Alexander said he was feeling sick, and because I was cross I ignored him. Then you took him downstairs and got him a glass of water. I was so mean that day. Was I always like that?'

A few months ago we were out for coffee and she said: 'I should never have let you take sips of alcohol when you were children.'

'But Mum, it was only on a few occasions, and we hated it,' I said.

'Still, I shouldn't have given it to you. Someone told me that was one of the reasons young people start drinking.'

My parents had given us everything: time, money, education, independence, experiences, and so much love. It was unconscionable to think that Alexander's death was in any way their fault, but all three of us wanted someone to blame. They let me have that, too. For a few years I couldn't be near Dad without exploding in anger over any trivial thing. 'You have to stop yelling at your dad,' Grandma told me one night. Only I couldn't.

Patrick shook me out of my rage. He said to me: 'It's a shit hand to be dealt but it's happened. You can either live the rest of your life miserable and hating each other, or you can pick yourself up—there's nothing that can be changed. He's not going to come walking through the door.'

It was the beginning of 2011. At the same time I was compiling lists of trite parental offences, the alcohol debate was dominating public discussion yet again. It had flared periodically for as long as I had been of drinking age, for a variety of reasons. Someone was king hit and killed in a Fortitude Valley cab queue, so restrictions on pub and club opening hours were introduced. Alcopops were taxed, to try to prevent underage drinking. Drunken street violence in Melbourne had got out of hand.

This time debate centred on Alice Springs' Indigenous population and the 'rivers of grog' in the Northern Territory. I heard an interview between the Radio National *Breakfast* host, Fran Kelly, and the then Opposition Leader, Tony Abbott. They were discussing the price of alcohol in Alice Springs. A 750-millilitre bottle of wine was cheaper than a can of Coke. The Opposition Leader expressed his shock at seeing illegal daytime drinking during his most recent visit.

'But if you can get a drink for twenty-six cents or a whole bottle of wine for two dollars, doesn't something need to be done about that?' Kelly asked.

'But if the law says you are not allowed to drink in public places and people are, don't we have to enforce the law?' Abbott replied. 'If the law says there's to be no drinking in the riverbeds and the place is littered with wine casks, don't we have to enforce the law?'

Kelly persisted: 'If the locals are saying the cheap grog, the access to grog is one of the problems, shouldn't we go there, too?'

'Well, I'm not saying we shouldn't but you've got to enforce the existing law before you start bringing in tougher laws. If the law isn't enforced, what's the point of making it tougher? I think the basic problem is that we don't want to see policemen and rangers confronting Aboriginal people in the street and I regret to say that sometimes it might be necessary. It is no substitute for enforcement to pass ever more draconian laws.'

When my friends and I were going out in Melbourne we usually left home with travellers—wine or beer to drink on the way—and we drank on trams, on trains and in the city, all public areas where it is illegal to consume alcohol. We were never stopped by law enforcement and, if we had been, I doubt it would have deterred us from taking travellers the next time we went out. We often drank in the park during the day. It was warmer, and easier to gather more people around.

Listening to the debate about drinking in the Northern Territory, I couldn't help thinking that it seemed a waste of time and resources to arrest people for drinking in public—it was a cosmetic measure, a way of avoiding the underlying causes. If there was a problem with alcohol in a community, it made more sense to put prices up. It had always made sense to me to buy as much alcohol as possible if I thought it was cheap. Behavioural economics is more powerful than police oversight.

I found it strange that one part of society was targeted by media and government, and expected to curtail their drinking, when most of the cultural cues in Australia emphasised the opposite. Everyone was exposed to the same sporting heroes touting the same alcoholic beverages—the same ads celebrating the same virtues of liquor. Everyone walked past the same retail outlets with the same cheap beverages; we all belonged to a community where alcohol was celebrated as an important part of social occasions, leisure activities and coming of age. The pub featured in music, film and almost every Australian television drama. Public figures who drank, including top politicians and sports people, were lauded: Bob Hawke and his schooner at the Sydney Cricket Ground epitomised the ideal. Almost two years after that radio interview with Fran Kelly, Tony Abbott, then on his way to the government backbench after a brief prime ministership, threw a final party for his colleagues and a marble table was broken in the drunken debauchery.

The difference between the people I knew who were big drinkers and the people in Alice Springs was that our European heritage, our white skin, on the whole gave us unearned social privileges—even if we were just as drunk. And, because the drinking problem was always discussed as a problem of others, we didn't think it affected us. Yet Alexander was a middle-class white kid midway through a higher-education degree when he died.

In 1986 the National Campaign Against Drug Abuse presented a National Alcohol Policy recommending the regulation of advertising and marketing, pricing and taxation, and availability of alcohol in Australia. This was supported by strong evidence that showed alcohol problems were related to consumption across a population. State governments, wary of getting the powerful liquor industry offside, decided against incorporating programs across the whole population, instead targeting minors, drink drivers and Indigenous people, even though the final policy document noted that strategies targeting only minority groups would be ineffective in tackling a population-wide health problem.

In Australia, each week one person aged between sixteen and twenty-five dies, and approximately sixty people aged between sixteen and twenty-five are hospitalised, because of an alcohol-related incident. A 2010 study jointly commissioned by VicHealth, Turning Point Alcohol and Drug Centre, and the Foundation for Alcohol Research and Education (FARE) found that fifteen people die each day in Australia from alcohol-related health complications. After tobacco, alcohol is shown to cause the most drug-related deaths in the world.

A few nights after I had heard Fran Kelly and Tony Abbott on the radio, at the end of a drunken weekday evening, a friend and

I walked into a pizza shop to buy something greasy for our walk home. A group of four men in their early twenties started making homophobic remarks about my friend.

'Fuck off,' I said.

'Don't, El,' my friend said.

'Fuck you, bitch,' one of the men said.

'We're leaving,' my friend said, grabbing my elbow and pulling me outside.

On the pavement was an unconscious man in his late twenties. He was chunky, with short brown hair. He was on his back, his eyes were shut, and he was bleeding from his forehead. He hadn't been there when we walked into the pizza shop.

A woman knelt over him. 'Do you know this guy?' she asked.

'No—what happened?' my friend said.

'Someone just came up and hit him. They hit him and then they ran off.'

'Do you need us to call an ambulance?'

'No, I've called one. It's coming. It's okay.'

We walked on, shaken. 'That could have been you,' my friend said.

Patrick has no bone in the bottom part of his nose because it's been punched in so many times. The first few times were on the football field. Each time after that was a bar-room brawl.

I don't know how many times my parents drilled it into us: 'Be careful; don't drink too much; look after yourself.' And yet, time and again, they would scrape us bleeding and bruised off footpaths, deal with vomit in the car, bail my brothers out of jail, and help us up the stairs to bed.

Sometimes Mum would resort to desperate measures to control us. Once, when Alexander came home really drunk and was about to go out again, Mum said to him that she would call the police if he left the house. 'Thankfully, that stopped him,' she said. 'I don't know what I would have done if he'd gone.'

When I was eighteen, my dad, a surgeon, stitched my chin up on the kitchen table at 1 a.m. after I'd tripped and fallen on my face. I had been chugging cheap warm champagne from the bottle. I was fully anaesthetised. I knew nothing of the incident until the next day, when I woke up with a gauze pad taped to my face.

When he was twenty-one, Patrick was arrested after a drunken scuffle. He woke up the next day in a watch house, with no memory of what happened or how he got there.

Patrick is studying to be a nurse, and he's good at it. He's funny and generous and kind—the kind of person other people warm to instantly. He was devastated by the incident. 'One minute you're there, and the next minute you wake up with a hangover and a black spot and everything's gone for you,' he said to me one evening in 2013.

'When we talk about it,' he said, 'I think: I do have a problem. But I've never really looked at it like that, 'cause if I have a problem then every single person who I hang out with has the same problem. I guess that's just the lifestyle that we live.'

'When did you start drinking?' I asked him.

'I was twelve or thirteen.'

He had hidden it from me. I didn't know he had started so young.

'I was rebellious, but it was probably the sort of environment I was in. There were girls around and it was easier to talk to them when I was drunk. And there was you.' He kind of skipped over the last part, but I figured what he meant was: that was what you were doing.

Maybe Patrick was still following me when we got older, only I was too wrapped up in myself to notice.

Like Patrick, it never occurred to me that I had a problem with drinking or that Alexander had a problem with drinking or that anyone I knew had a problem with drinking, despite the many incidents that indicated we did. The way we drank was just how everybody we knew drank. It certainly never occurred to me that my drinking might have influenced my brothers' behaviour.

For the first time since Alexander died my anger had a worthy recipient, and it was uncomfortable. How might it have been different if, instead of laughing at my brother's drunken exploits, I had been alarmed by them?

15

ONE PUNCH

Half an hour before midnight my friend Jonathan (not his real name) and I were queuing for the ATM. We'd been waiting for ten minutes, but there were still three people in front of us and I had to piss. Jonathan was sucking on a cigarette and telling me about his jacket; I was jiggling to keep my bladder shut.

'I fought for this jacket. There were three other people running for the hanger and…Oh, fuck.'

At the front of the queue a girl said, 'Oops, it wasn't me,' and walked off. We stared at the winding cartoon cogs on the out-of-service screen. The people in the queue grew fractious. Small blisters of anger rose and popped.

The boy behind us muttered, 'What the fuck—why is this

taking so long?' He was about eighteen, with a face like freshly risen dough glazed in sugar syrup. Muted freckles were spattered across his button nose.

'It's going to take a lot longer now that the ATM is broken,' Jonathan snapped.

'What the fuck, dude?' the boy said. 'Why the fuck are you talking like that?'

'What's wrong?' I asked.

'Why is your friend talking to me like that?'

'Like what?'

'He's all like, *It's going to take a lot longer now that the ATM is broken.*' The boy mimicked Jonathan in a high-pitched voice.

'It's okay,' I said. 'We want to use the ATM, too. He's not angry at you—he's angry at the machine.'

'Well—he shouldn't fucking speak like that.'

I was about to say something, but Jonathan looked at me. 'Don't,' he mouthed, shaking his head.

When we were younger, and out late at night, Jonathan would say: 'Just so you know, if someone tries to attack us, I will run. I will leave you.'

I laughed the first time he said it. Then I realised he was serious.

'Really?'

'Yes. It would be best if you ran as well.'

He often said it in the early morning, when we were half cut, walking down a dark street in Fortitude Valley. 'What about right now?' I'd ask, trotting to keep up with him. 'Would you leave me now?'

'Yes,' he'd say, striding ahead, looking at the pavement. 'You're not the one who's going to get punched in the face.'

'What if you left me and I was raped?'

'The point is, you have to run too, El. Just be glad I told you, and it's not a surprise.'

I went to preschool with Jonathan. At the party for his fifth birthday there was a magician who pulled a dove out of a hat, and a rope made of hundreds of knotted coloured scarves out of his sleeve. So many scarves it seemed they would never stop. I couldn't figure out where he fitted them: it was as if his insides were stuffed with coloured scarves, and he was slowly unravelling his nervous system.

Back then Jonathan was small, round and unusually polite. The last of these traits made him appear old-fashioned at five. Now he is six foot three, with broad shoulders. He has grown into his politeness. He is witty and impossibly charming.

Because I've never entirely believed Jonathan's late-night warning, I laugh in mock disbelief when I tell people about it. Usually, my audience laughs, too. Lately, though, I've told a few people who haven't smiled. Instead, they have said: 'That would be the right thing to do.'

Jonathan and I have never been attacked. He did, however, have to run once, last year. He was at a show in a venue on Ann Street, in Fortitude Valley: a dark, cavernous space, up a black staircase. Jonathan only knew the musician by reputation and had never heard him, but someone had put his name on the door. Halfway through the main act he became bored, and began making snide remarks.

He told me he wasn't talking loudly. At least, he didn't think he was. But, nearby, a thin man with a record in his fist and a canvas satchel over his shoulder was getting angry. 'When I turned around, I accidentally caught his eye. He looked at me and barked, "Show some fucking respect or shut up," then he rushed me,' Jonathan said. 'He was really drunk.'

Jonathan grabbed his companion by the arm, yelled, 'Run!' and they pushed their way through the crowd and down the stairs. Outside, on the street, they lit cigarettes with shaky hands, and sucked the smoke in deep to compose themselves.

The incident shook him. 'It was terrifying, El,' he told me. 'I actually felt afraid for my safety. I've never experienced that before.'

A few weeks after Jonathan ran out of the show he sent me a text. 'I'm at the Boundary Hotel and someone's just been glassed in the bathroom. There's blood everywhere.' It was a weeknight, around 10.30. This time Jonathan's mouth had nothing to do with it.

The recently refurbished Boundary Hotel is roughly halfway along the main street of a rapidly gentrifying inner-city suburb. In its renovated wooden beer garden, Wagyu beef burgers and Atlantic salmon are served alongside boutique ciders and ales. My friend's mum met her partner in the front bar a couple of years ago, and on Sunday afternoons there's live bluegrass.

It may have been the location, the image of watery blood on dirty tiles, or my inability to envisage what could get someone worked up enough to cut a person before 12 p.m. on a school night, but I was shocked.

Each night I get two Google alert emails. One lists the top ten trending articles for the day containing the keyword 'drunk' and the other the top ten containing 'alcohol'.

I subscribed to the alerts at the end of February 2014, about two months after eighteen-year-old Daniel Christie was killed by a single blow on Victoria Street in Kings Cross, Sydney. His attacker, Shaun McNeill, had punched another youth in the head. Christie confronted him about it, and McNeill punched Christie in the head, causing him to fall and fatally crack his skull on the pavement.

The unprovoked attack was the second of its kind in two months. The other fatality was a twenty-three-year-old Irishman, Thomas Jay Keaney, who was on the phone to his mum when he was drunkenly attacked and killed in Perth. Although Keaney's death quickly slipped from the public eye, Christie's lit a fire. The sustained attention it received seemed emblematic of heightened community concern about alcohol abuse in Australia.

Between 2000 and 2014, there were ninety-one fatal one-punch attacks in Australia. Of these, only Christie and Keaney's deaths occurred between December 2013 and January 2014: the summer was not abnormally violent. But the deaths happened at the end of a year during which public awareness about Australia's binge-drinking culture had been stoked by numerous television and radio documentaries on the subject. Christie's family were outspoken about the need for tougher alcohol restrictions, and called on media outlets to use the term 'coward punch' rather than 'king hit' for such attacks.

At the time Christie was killed, Kieran Loveridge, the man

charged with the one-punch death of eighteen-year-old Thomas Kelly in 2012, was appealing his manslaughter charge. Christie's and Kelly's deaths were similar. Both had been attacked in Kings Cross. Neither victim had provoked their attacker. Both perpetrators had been drinking. Shaun MacNeill was alleged to have drunk eight beers and a glass of wine over six hours, while Kieran Loveridge had drunk six double-strength Smirnoff Blacks in under two hours—each can was equivalent to almost two standard drinks.

Following the death of Daniel Christie, Thomas Kelly's family presented the state government with a petition signed by 140,000 people calling for tougher sentencing for one-punch offenders. The petition resulted in the introduction of mandatory sentencing for one-punch killers in New South Wales, Queensland and, most recently, Victoria. Rather than shortening his sentence, Loveridge's appeal led to his charge being upgraded from manslaughter to murder.

A week after Christie's death the federal Minister for Indigenous Affairs, Nigel Scullion, announced a parliamentary inquiry into alcohol-fuelled violence. The inquiry, he said, would not be 'fenced off on racial grounds', as it was a problem that 'concerned all Australians'. A day later he said the inquiry would be into alcohol-related problems in Indigenous communities only.

In February 2014 the federal Minister for Health, Fiona Nash, announced plans to scrap funding for the Alcohol and Other Drugs Council of Australia, the Australian government's alcohol and drug advisory board. She was too busy to meet with representatives to explain why the funding was being cut, but the week the news broke she met with the alcohol industry's safe-drinking body, Drink Wise, twice.

The diversity and inconsistency of news about alcohol abuse in Australia was especially stark around this period. The difference in opinion centred on whether the alcohol industry was the problem, or whether a few violent individuals were responsible for ruining nights out.

In the *Australian*, the Swinburne and Monash university public-health and human-psychopharmacology academic Mike Keane railed against the alcohol restrictions promoted by many of his colleagues:

> We must, for the safety of our children, address the increasing problem of violent street assaults. And for our society's sake, we must not listen to the self-serving, narrowly focused, ideologically driven posturing of our out-of-touch elitist public health advocates...Many of us have been drunk in our time; alcohol doesn't cause violence. Thus, instead of demonising the enjoyable use of alcohol with bans on advertising and so on, we should refocus our efforts on ruthlessly taking violent thugs out of circulation; and by doing so, gradually reducing the cultural appeal of violence.

On the other side of the argument, an op-ed in the Melbourne *Age* by the CEO of Anglicare, Paul McDonald, called for the minimum ten-year sentence for one-punch attacks to be reduced: 'all of the recent "one-punch fatalities" in Victoria have involved alcohol in some way. Yet governments only seem concerned with the harm caused by the individual and not the harm caused by the product.'

Dr Anthony Lynham, an energetic, jovial man with a bright gaze, is on the side of the public-health campaigners. In 2014 he quit his job as an oral and maxillofacial surgeon at the Royal Brisbane Hospital to contend the state seat of Stafford as a Labor candidate, promising to tackle alcohol-related violence. He won a landslide victory.

In 2013, when he was still working as a surgeon, Dr Lynham told me that he became interested in alcohol reform when he noticed the number of facial fractures caused by drunken violence were increasing. Each year he estimated his hospital unit saw just under nine hundred cases, and of those close to half were the result of alcohol-related violence. For patients aged eighteen to twenty-one it was more than three-quarters. The injuries were typically a broken cheek, jawbone or eye socket.

Oral and maxillofacial registrars at the hospital were among the best oral-trauma surgeons in Australia, Dr Lynham explained, but some of the least experienced at general oral surgery because they were only seeing trauma victims. 'I thought it was just us when I first looked at the data,' he said. 'That's why I looked at it because I thought: Wow—this is really starting to be a bit of a concern. What the hell's going on?'

He ran through a litany of incidents that brought patients to the hospital. 'There's the girl who was walking back from a bar with some drinks and brushed another girl's drink. The second girl's drink spilt, so she punched the first girl in the face and broke her cheekbone. Then we had the case of Joshua—he was in a nightclub and he was just dancing with his girlfriend; a guy tried to suggest that the girlfriend dance with him, and Josh said,

"Oh, no, she's dancing with me," and then *whack!* With no provocation whatsoever.' He punched his hand into his palm.

My friend Patrick McAnelly—a former worker at the now-defunct Surfers Paradise Chill Out Zone, a space for individuals having a bad experience with alcohol or drugs—told me a few years ago, 'There's nothing worse than seeing the shock of people the first time they are confronted by extreme violence; it's a terrible thing to watch. They generally take half an hour, then they are really affected. These are men, and not always young men, who've joked, or said the wrong thing, or laughed in a bar, or outside a bar, or in the street, and because of that they have been headbutted three times and split by massive, strong younger or older men—doesn't matter. And they're angry at first, then you clean them up and you see that their whole reality has been altered.'

In February 2014 laws restricting bottle-shop, pub and club trading hours in Sydney city hotspots—including Kings Cross, Darlinghurst, The Rocks and Haymarket—were introduced. The lockout laws placed no restrictions on the nearby casino's trading hours.

These laws were welcomed by most public-health advocates. But, as Dr Michael Livingston noted in the FARE publication *Stemming the Tide of Alcohol*, while they were effective, they also diverted attention from the concerning expansion of packaged-liquor outlets, which sell four-fifths of all alcohol, which are increasingly owned by the major supermarket chains, and which are indirectly responsible for more insidious and widespread harm: family violence and alcohol-specific chronic disease.

Meanwhile, the pubs and bars in Sydney's lockout zone started to close. In a LinkedIn article that went viral, 'Would the last person in Sydney please turn the lights out?', the chief executive of Freelancer.com, Matt Barrie, argued: 'As I write this in 2016, not a day goes by without the press reporting of yet another bar, club, hotel, restaurant or venue closing...The soul of the city has been destroyed.'

In 2010, following the introduction of a trial of similar lockout laws in Victoria, The Tote in Collingwood, Melbourne, announced that it was closing because the then owner, Bruce Milne, couldn't afford the licensing conditions. Liquor-licensing laws had been changed in reaction to a spate of drunken violence in the city. The Tote had long been an iconic live-music venue. Reaction to the announcement was swift—around two thousand protestors rallied around the building to voice their dissent, and the pub was saved from closure when Seventh Tipple bought it.

Today, The Tote puts on about 750 bands each year. As its owner, Jon Perring, explained to me, 'Live music and alcohol goes back forever, so the regulation of the liquor industry—where it oversteps the line—impacts on the art form.'

A good friend of mine who manages a live-music venue in the adjoining suburb of Fitzroy said: 'On a good night I feel like I'm getting paid to hang out with friends and watch great bands. For the most part I feel like I'm part of an institution that has a positive influence.

'My favourite nights are when the bar is full of familiar faces who are there to see a local band. My worst experiences have involved customers who have become violent. Thankfully such incidents are very rare at our venue.'

At a family wedding a few years ago, Patrick turned to me and said, 'In your book, will you write about this?' I looked where he was pointing and saw my mum, aunts, uncles, cousins and second cousins laughing and dancing like idiots, not caring what anybody thought. They were tipsy and gorgeous in the low lights on the dance floor. 'You have to write about the good side of alcohol, too,' he said.

Alcohol fuels the dark, sticky pubs that keep live music going, and it's these small businesses, not the big players in the industry, whose existence is usually threatened when governments bring in legislation to restrict the sale and consumption of alcohol. I feel conflicted about the demise of Sydney's nightlife—something that will possibly happen in Brisbane when similar lockout laws come into effect in 2016—and I agree with much of Matt Barrie's article. But midway through it there is a line that stuck, that I couldn't move past, and like a canker it rotted some of his reasoning for me:

> Two young men would be turning in their graves if they knew that their deaths had been hijacked to beat up some moral outrage over the sort of human tragedy that sells newspapers to put up a political smokescreen, push a prohibitionist evangelical agenda, sell a suburb to developers and boost the coffers of a couple of casinos.

It was a carefully worded statement, designed to make readers scoff at some of the moralistic ways in which Thomas Kelly and Daniel Christie had been used as leverage to enact Sydney's lockout laws—it was not meant to disrespect or diminish the tragedy of their deaths. And yes, maybe those two young men would be turning in their graves—I sometimes wonder if Alexander might be doing the same. Only it's not just about those two young men: it's about all the people they left behind.

16

WHEN MATTHEW STANLEY DIED

Paul Stanley's son Matthew was killed in a one-punch attack in September 2006. He and three of his friends were at an eighteenth-birthday party when it started to get violent, and they left. Although they were supposed to call Paul to pick them up, the four boys decided to walk home. On the way out, they stopped on the footpath and Matthew started talking to one of his female friends. The guy who was getting violent inside suddenly fronted him. Matthew looked up. 'Mate, I'm just going,' he said.

That was all he got out before the guy punched him in the face and he crumpled. When he was laid out on the ground the guy started kicking him, then slammed his knee into his chest. The perpetrator weighed 105 kilograms. Matthew, aged fifteen, was a little grommet. The attack left him with two fractures to the skull, four broken ribs and a crushed lung.

Thirty seconds after Matthew was hit, someone called 000. The incident was designated code one, most urgent, and an ambulance was dispatched immediately. One minute after Matt was hit, someone else called an ambulance. The dispatcher heard swearing and yelling in the background, so he contacted the ambulance that was heading to the scene and downgraded the urgency level to code three. One minute and thirty seconds after the attack, the neighbours called the police to report a street riot. The police contacted the ambulance service, and the dispatcher contacted the ambulance. He told the paramedics to pull over until they had confirmation that it was safe to continue.

Forty-seven minutes after the first call, the ambulance arrived at the scene. Paul and his wife, Kay, had driven past it on the side of the road on their way to pick up Matthew. Paul told me that they didn't know why it was sitting there.

When I met him, Paul said to me, 'I've got a phone message from an ex-coroner who says he knows the story and the length of time Matthew was on the ground. He's enquired and he says, with the type of injuries Matt received, if the ambulance had got there a minute after he was punched he probably wouldn't have survived. But that being said—maybe he would have.'

Paul makes a point of calling it murder, although the sixteen-year-old perpetrator was charged with manslaughter. He'd drunk sixteen bourbon and cokes before he punched Matt, and it couldn't be proven that his actions were those of someone with full capacity of his senses.

'He was a large person, he was violent and he was drunk,' Paul told me. 'You put alcohol and a violent person together, and there's going to be trouble. It's the same old thing. What I try to tell kids is, you can actually have fun in life without being full as a boot on alcohol.'

Matthew was still breathing when the ambulance arrived, but he was brain dead. The next day his life support was switched off.

The Stanley family had to wait two weeks before they could bury Matthew so the coroner could conduct an autopsy. Paul Stanley isn't religious—he told me that if he didn't believe in God before Matthew's death, he certainly wasn't going to believe after it—but while they were waiting a local priest contacted him. A number of Matthew's school friends were this priest's parishioners and he asked the Stanleys if they would consider having the funeral service in his church.

The Stanleys agreed to look at the church. 'It was huge,' Paul said. There was space for 480 people in the main auditorium and an option to have the service streamed on CCTV to side rooms. 'How many people do you think will be coming, mate?' Paul asked, incredulously.

'Matthew had a lot of friends,' the priest replied. He was right: more than a thousand people filled the church for the funeral.

The priest told Paul to call him the Preacher Man. 'The Preacher Man saved my life,' Paul said. 'Without him, I'd be hanging from a tree somewhere.'

Before Matthew's death Paul was a father and a small-business owner. He specialised in putting coating on vinyl flooring and was heavily involved in his kids' sport. After Matthew died he became the CEO and spokesman of the Matthew Stanley Foundation. The main part of his role is giving talks at schools around the country about what happened to his son.

Paul is tall and thin, with a thatch of steel-grey hair. He doesn't so much tell stories as exude them. They're compelling and powerful, and they flow from one to another seamlessly. I can imagine why he might have an affinity with a preacher man.

Paul greeted me one sunny winter afternoon at the door of his family home, in a comfortable middle-class suburb about forty-five minutes from Brisbane's city centre. He was wearing a Matthew Stanley Foundation T-shirt and wristbands. At his feet was a fluffy dog named Bailey, after his wife's favourite drink. 'If I got to name him after my favourite drink, he'd have been called Beer,' Paul said, and I laughed awkwardly because I was nervous.

He showed me inside. The house was the always-clean type, not the type where mess is hurriedly stuffed into cupboards and spare rooms in anticipation of a visitor. We sat on comfortable black leather couches in the front room. Unbidden, Paul started talking. He asked me about my brother, told me about the changes in his suburb and filled me in on the work of the Matthew Stanley Foundation.

Paul started the foundation three months after Matthew died because he and his wife wanted something good to come out of his death. The foundation began with a mix of Matt's friends and adults visiting shopping centres to hand out Queensland Police

'Party Safe' brochures. Then someone asked Paul to give a talk, and it took off from there. He told me that in the past five and a half years he had spoken to more than 150,000 school children. When I met with him in 2013 he had just come back from talks in Townsville and was about to go to Charleville.

Paul ran me through a typical presentation. At the start he shows a compilation of the TV stories about Matthew's death. When the clips finish he walks onto the stage. 'The kids go: Wow, he's the guy who was just on the TV,' he said.

I asked what happens next. 'I just tell everybody exactly what happened right through, and get as graphic as I possibly can and as confrontational as I possibly can. When that finishes we talk about the Walk Away Chill Out thing.'

The Matthew Stanley foundation started the Walk Away Chill Out campaign in 2011 in an attempt to address drunken teen violence. Paul also travels with a race-car team called No Second Chance, which is another avenue for telling Matthew's story. The main message of his talk is not to be scared of walking away from a violent incident.

'I tell them: If walking doesn't work, run. If you're the person who's going to be the victim, run like hell, as fast as you possibly can. If you're going to be the perpetrator, take a step back. Because nothing in your life is worth dying for. Matthew went to a party to have fun with his friends. He didn't go to die, but he did.'

Paul still cries when he tells the story. 'I'm standing in front of a room of three hundred and fifty Year Eleven and Twelve students with tears rolling down my cheek. Or I have to stop because I'm choking in the throat, and the kids acknowledge that. They understand; they get an idea of what it's all about. The horror of losing someone close to you.'

Paul is gruff but warm, and I found myself telling him things about my family and my brother that I usually only tell people I know. It often happens to him after his talks. He told me about a young man who came up to him and confessed that he'd assaulted someone. He told me about listening to the little girl who came up to him and said her father had died. He told me about the young man who asked if he could speak to him because he had anger-management issues. 'Every day before school I stand outside and I punch the pole,' he said, and showed Paul a swollen, bruised hand.

'I think you'd better get that looked at,' Paul said. 'But first, let's talk.' They sat in the middle of the school gymnasium and Paul missed his plane home so he could listen to the kid's story. He seems indiscriminately generous with his time and his anecdotes, his ear and his advice.

But there was, too, something almost evangelical about Paul's zeal for sharing Matthew's story. He carried his son's death around like a globe on his shoulders. It sustained him, it gave him purpose, but it also seemed stultifying.

About ten minutes after we sat down a car started outside. 'That's Nick, my other son,' Paul said. 'Today's the first time I've seen him for three weeks. He won't come and say goodbye to me when he's here. He just sneaks out the back.' And then, with characteristic openness, he started talking about the troubles he was having with Nick. I was surprised at how frank Paul was with a stranger—and more surprised at the contrast between his stories about connecting with the kids he spoke to, all strangers, and the disconnect with his living son. I wondered what it must be like to live in the shadow of your dad's obsession with your older brother and his death.

Later, Paul said, 'The person who was probably most affected was Nicholas. That's the end result of Matthew's murder. And a lot of Nicholas's attitude to life now can be laid at Kay's and my feet, because we didn't know what to do. What I say to people is, "Your son or your daughter has died in tragic circumstances. Yes. How many times a day do you tell your other child that you love them? Ten? It's not enough. Tell them thirty times."

'People come around and they want to talk about your brother, Alexander, or my son. They don't want to talk about you, because you're here. They don't want to talk about Nicholas, because he's here.'

When I asked him about his son's killer, Paul bridled. The anger was still raw. 'He came out of jail. I had been told that he was going to be deported, because six months before he was served with a notion of intention to deport, and that gives them six months to actually lodge an appeal. On the day he was released they just opened the gate, he got into the car with his aunty and uncle and two cousins, and they came back to nearby Capalaba to live happily ever after. And for me to go and see friends of ours I had to drive past the house, so I just said to them, "The only time I'll see you is if you come round here. I just don't trust myself driving past his house." But he got the message fairly rapidly that his presence was not exactly welcome around here.'

'I don't get it,' I wanted to say. 'Who's your organisation for if not for people like him?' But what would I know? I have no idea how it feels to lose someone I love to senseless violence. And how could I have said it? Paul Stanley's anger blared like a foghorn through the thick smog of his pain and shock.

After a couple of minutes, he asked: 'How many years is it since your brother died?'

'He died at the end of 2009,' I said.

'That's coming up four years and you're crying. It's seven years at the end of this year [since Matthew died] and I'm regularly crying. It doesn't go away. And that's still what I'm saying to people. You become capable of handling it. Handling your grief. And I say to people: "Don't be scared of crying. Don't hold back crying all the time. You're allowed to, for God's sake. You're allowed to and you should be. Those tears—you are honouring the person you're thinking about. You're doing them an honour, because you care." And Matthew's up there looking down. He's sitting on my shoulder. And he's looking down and he knows those tears are for him. A boy you never even heard of and you're crying for him. Here you are crying about someone you never even met.'

A few months after Alexander died I was at a party and a friend came up to ask how I was doing. 'I'm okay,' I said.

'I think of you all the time,' the friend said. We were standing next to a table decorated with tea candles. The friend picked one up. He was pissed and swaying slightly. 'I'll light a candle for your mum,' he said, staring at me.

'Okay,' I said as he put the lit candle on the table.

'I'll light a candle for Paddy. This candle is for your dad.' He put the candles next to each other on the table.

'Yeah, cool, thanks,' I said and tried to walk away.

'This one's for you,' he said, flicking his thumb down on the lighter, 'and this one is for Alex.'

I started to cry. For a second I swear he looked triumphant. The thought of being emotionally manipulated made me seethe.

Paul was doing the same thing, I thought. But it was powerful, and I fell for it; I was crying. And when I listen back to the recording of our interview, I hear how I'm polite, acquiescent. 'Yes,' I say.

It's my tactic, too, I realise later. I know that often I'm not just trying to make people see the follies, the inconsistencies, the pitfalls of the way we use alcohol. I also tell Alexander's story because I am flaunting my grief. 'Look at it!' I want to shout. 'Feel and touch and taste this terrible thing that has happened to me.' Like a drinker craving companionship, I can't grieve alone. I need to be shored up by other people's pity, their awe. 'I don't know how you can do what you're doing,' people say to me.

'It's important,' I answer—sometimes because I believe it, sometimes smugly.

I need them, because I'm stuck. I got stuck in Alexander's death, like Paul Stanley is stuck in Matthew's death, with this terrible, awesome shock that resounds over the years.

This is what we do. We retell our stories, trying to find a way to maximise the impact. If I cut a word here, will it sound sadder? If I move this section? Paul and I both use our stories to elicit emotion, to force a reaction.

But there's pain in that, too. Towards the end of the first hour of the interview Paul said to me, 'Without [Matthew] being with me I wouldn't be able to do the presentations that I do. I definitely have to sit on my own—well, the two of us together—before I do a presentation, because I have to psych myself up for it. And then when I'm ready to do it, that's when the game face comes on.

'I collapsed on stage one time. I was talking at a school to a whole lot of Year Twelve kids, and I started saying how pleased and proud your mum and dad would be when you get nice and dressed up to go to your school formal, and that sort of stuff, and I kept getting flashes of Matty, and then next thing I was outside the hall with two coppers standing holding me up, and they said I was talking away and then I stopped talking and went into la-la land and they realised something had happened, and they came up and helped me out. And the headmaster of the school said to me afterwards: "You should finish your presentation like that every time. The kids were just..." [He makes a face of awe.] And I said, "Yeah, I could do that." Only trouble was, I didn't know what I did.'

I understood this. Telling the story of people close to you who have died is tiring.

I talked to Paul Stanley for two and a half hours. By the end of the interview I was exhausted, and I think he was as well.

Paul walked me to the curb. Out on the lawn the lively, warm storyteller was gone. In his place was a tall, slightly deflated man with grey hair and lolly-coloured wristbands. His face was stern again. It had been such an intense conversation, for me at least, that I wondered if he would hug me. He didn't. He said a curt goodbye. 'Good luck, and if you need anything, please call. What you're doing is so important.'

I was holding a magazine that he gave me just before we left the house. The cover is a picture of Matthew Stanley, all messy blond hair, squinting blue eyes, spotty teenage skin and the slightly arrogant smile of a cute fifteen-year-old boy who knows he's popular and clever, his parents love him, his dad is strong and tall.

I kept the magazine in my cupboard for a while. I meant to read the article about Matthew; only, each time I tried, I stopped after the first few paragraphs. Eventually I put the magazine in a hanging file under my bed. I couldn't look at Matthew's face anymore. It made me too sad.

Matthew Stanley's death feels like a horrible aberration. I keep thinking about the twisted bodies in Pompeii, trapped forever in their daily tasks. When Matthew died it must have been like a volcano exploding in that family. I imagine Paul looking around, his face a mask of grief and shock before the wave of lava bore down and he petrified in his pain.

'It's alcohol,' Paul had said to me. 'You've just got to think before you act, and the first part of thinking is when you're pouring the next lot of alcohol down your neck.' It seemed so simple when he said it.

17
LITTLE BROWN JUG

In primary school, on Tuesday afternoons, our class filed through the sick bay and up the stairs to the hall stage where our ruddy-cheeked library teacher sat waiting at a honky off-key piano, her bright pink lips curved into a staged grin. When we were seated she flicked on the overhead projector, then began to pound on the piano with non-musical fervour. We whispered, played with each other's hair, slid around the floor and sometimes sang, all the while with one eye on her back.

The library teacher would become unpredictably hysterical—once, during a lesson on how to read the phonebook, she whacked the head of the girl sitting next to me with a drumstick for no reason that we could discern—and, because of this, a restless energy permeated her classes as we nervously, gleefully anticipated the action that would make her snap.

The only time the class reached some form of harmony was when she played 'Little Brown Jug', a robust drinking ditty from the 1800s, which united us in a way 'Flying Purple People Eater', 'Mairzy Doats' and 'Ghost of Tom' did not. It was by far her most requested song. At the first few bars, Ricky ceased rolling on the floor with his shirt around his nipples, the older boys halted their sliding from one side of the stage to the other and the whispering died down.

The lyrics describe an alcoholic couple living alone in a log hut; the narrator is the husband. Despite the couple's dull existence and diverse tastes—she loves gin and he loves rum—they use the same vessel, a little brown jug, for their drink, and in it find a shared solace. The chorus, which we shouted, is: 'Ha ha ha, you and me, little brown jug don't I love thee.'

We sang it, unremarked upon, for years, but in Grade Six we wised up to lines like 'The rose is red, my nose is too' and 'If I'd a cow that gave such milk, I'd dress her in the finest silk', and 'Little Brown Jug' was suddenly wonderfully illicit.

The primary school was Catholic. In Grade Two we learned how Jesus turned water into wine at the Canaan party; each year we fidgeted on the scratchy brown church carpet at Easter while the priest read Jesus' denunciation of earthly fermented substances during his last supper; and later, once I had made my first communion, I drank his transubstantiated blood—a mouthful of spit-flecked port—on Sundays.

But while Jesus' wine drinking was an essential, almost dull, part of his holy identity, and he never got drunk, the protagonist in 'Little Brown Jug' was different: looser and more exotic. To primary-school children subject to bedtimes, censorship, diet control and constricted travel, a song about alcoholism was a flying pig. We delighted in its unlikeliness, and the library teacher delighted in its ability to control us for a few minutes.

In this way, even the suggestion of alcohol saw us unwittingly subject to some of its most distinctive properties: it gave us pleasure, it broke down social barriers and it united us in a common purpose.

It is not known how or exactly when humans learned to exploit yeast to make liquor, but at some point it was developed in every society where fruit, grain or vegetables were available. The anthropologist Anne Fox suggests that humans use alcohol as a salve for the unease created by human advancement: 'It is part of our illusion and self-delusion to deal with a changed world.'

During the Neolithic era, when many human groups transitioned from hunter-gatherer societies to farming societies, grapes, grains and cereals such as rice, barley and wheat were domesticated. With the domestication of crops regular alcohol production was assured; beer was invented and wine refined. Alcohol was an antidote to the boredom of backbreaking agricultural work and the submissions of a newly hierarchical society.

As human societies grew bigger drunkenness alleviated some of the problems caused by living further away from the tight-knit communities we used to inhabit. Alcohol decreases an individual's ability to deceive and detect deception, prevents us from picking up on fear cues, and allows us to converse without anxiety. It creates a euphoric state, characterised by lack of inhibition, happiness and a diminished sense of risk. However, drunkenness also causes problems and, in recognition of its potency, most cultures and religions designed rituals, laws and customs to regulate alcohol intake.

In 1969 Craig MacAndrew and Robert B. Edgerton published *Drunken Comportment*, a survey of drinking ranging from Bolivia to Tahiti. MacAndrew and Edgerton came to the conclusion that 'persons learn about drunkenness what their societies impart to them, and comporting themselves in consonance with these understandings they become living confirmations of their societies' teachings.' The book ends: 'Since societies, like individuals, get the sorts of drunken comportment that they allow, they deserve what they get.'

As Donald Horne observed in 1964, in *The Lucky Country*, 'Australians have never been quite the nation of boozers they imagine themselves to be'—and we're still not. Australia ranks equal fifteenth with Switzerland and the United Kingdom on the list of countries with the highest annual alcohol consumption per capita. According to the Australian Bureau of Statistics, in 2012–13 Australians drank 9.9 litres of alcohol per person, per annum. This is the lowest level since the mid-1990s. Fewer people are drinking beer and wine consumption is levelling out.

Yet there is something unsettling and unsettled about the place of alcohol in Australian society. At its best the drinking culture is characterised by egalitarianism, a laidback attitude and a spirit of creativity. Australians invented the goon bag and the stubby, while the first tubs of Vegemite were by-products of discarded Carlton and United Brewery yeast. At its worst the nation's drinking can be characterised by violent recklessness, exclusion and a pattern of boozing to extremes.

Among people who do drink, those who drink to the most harmful levels are consuming more alcohol than before. In 2013, one-fifth of consumers drank three-quarters of all alcohol consumed. FARE notes that, each year, '70,000 Australians are victims of alcohol-related assaults, including 24,000 victims of alcohol-related domestic violence. All these harms cost the nation an estimated $36 billion annually.'

In mid-2013 I interviewed Dr Mark Daglish, at the time a senior lecturer in Drug and Alcohol Studies at the University of Queensland. Dr Daglish is a short Scottish psychiatrist with an impressive moustache. I met him in his rooms at the Royal Brisbane and Women's Hospital, where he's the director of Addiction Psychiatry.

'There's no doubt that Australia has an alcohol problem,' he told me. 'I mean, you only have to look at the number of people coming through the emergency departments with alcohol-related injuries or illnesses, whether that's a side effect or adverse events from a single episode of heavy drinking, a single episode of somebody else's heavy drinking or problems from long-term heavy consumption.

'Alcohol in small amounts is not that harmful,' he said, 'but then there's the social constructs, most of which are now geared towards not allowing you to stop at a small amount. The relative price has come down; the marketing is all geared around wild nights and fun things. A lot of the environmental and structural things that used to contain risks—you couldn't afford to drink that much, the bars shut at 11.30, they were spread around and weren't condensed in one area—have been relaxed. So, now, if you've got a piece of plastic in your pocket you can stick it in a machine inside the bar. Maybe we need twelve-digit PINs.'

—

The year I turned nineteen I followed a man I loved to South Africa. One night we were driving along a dirt road skirting a beach on the country's east coast. He was behind the wheel and I was in the passenger seat. We had been fighting; he was smoking and I was smouldering with indignation. The windows were down and we were drunk. Neither of us was wearing a seatbelt; no one there did. The car was going fast, taking curves sharply, flying over small bumps and smacking back onto the gravel.

'Are you sure you should be driving?' I asked lamely, belatedly. 'You've been drinking.'

He turned slightly. 'Ilza-beth,' he snapped—he could never pronounce my name—'if I was too drunk to drive, you would know, because I would be vomiting out this window.'

'Okay,' I said, and we tore on through the night.

He had a friend—a blustery man, loud and congenial. I can't recall his name, and I find it difficult to picture his face. But his right leg I remember well. It was like a tube of toothpaste three-quarters empty. Not a tube that someone has squeezed carefully from the bottom, but a tube squeezed in random places, so that in some parts it is flat and in others it is plump. Scarred skin stretched tight across the bone like cling film. Where the skin was not scarred, small pillows of flesh popped out.

He'd been driving home drunk and had crashed the car. 'He was lucky,' the man I loved told me. Among his friends, luck was any incident that might have resulted in death but didn't. Except that the man who had crashed wasn't lucky. His leg was stuffed.

Back then, in that place, the people I was with drove drunk because nobody stopped them. Those who were lucky, including the man I loved and me, staggered out of the car at their intended destinations. Those who were unlucky did not.

I remember that night because it was anathema to what I knew. It was drilled into us, and had been for as long as I could remember, that we should not drink and drive. By 1988 all Australian states had implemented Random Breath Testing as a way of catching drivers with a blood-alcohol content over 0.05 per cent. From 1981 to 2006 the incidence of alcohol-related traffic accidents in Australia fell by more than one-third. Societies—drinking cultures—do change.

18

DRY

The year I started to talk about Alexander's death and its link to alcohol, which was the year I moved back to Brisbane, most conversations led to Chris Raine. Chris, who was then a Brisbane local, founded Hello Sunday Morning, an online organisation for Australians wanting to change their drinking habits. HSM members pledge to give up drinking for a period of time and blog about their experiences to a community of fellow abstainers.

HSM started in 2009 with Chris, an advertising professional, as its sole member. He was twenty-two and had been drinking since he was fourteen. The previous year he was challenged by an employer to come up with a way of dissuading young people from binge drinking. This got him thinking about his own drinking habits, and after a boozy New Year's Eve and a bad break-up he resolved to go sober for the rest of 2009, blogging about the experience every Sunday. By December twenty of his friends had signed up, too. Today, HSM has more than fifty thousand members.

While HSM is for alcohol abusers—weekend or weeknight binge drinkers—rather than alcoholics, its use of confessional storytelling and community support is similar to Alcoholics Anonymous. Unlike Alcoholics Anonymous, HSM is online, so it's possible to build rapport with many other community members. And, while anonymity is an option (members can choose a username that obscures their identity), it's not part of its ethos. In fact, HSM apparel—T-shirts, singlets and hoodies—is sold on the site, so you can choose to advertise your affiliation with the organisation.

The journalist Jill Stark was so inspired by an interview she conducted with Chris Raine that she embarked on her own yearlong sobriety challenge. In her 2013 memoir of the experience, *High Sobriety*, she wrote of him: 'Relentlessly upbeat and energetic, he had a passion for his work that coursed through him so violently he was practically luminous. Here was a man on a mission—to change our drinking culture and to unlock what he believed to be Australia's greatest untapped resource: Sunday mornings.'

In the years since his organisation began, Chris has been named the Young Queenslander of the Year, and he was a National Finalist for Young Australian of the Year. In 2013 he was awarded the prestigious (if, given his work with HSM, ironically named)

Skoll Scholarship to undertake a Master of Business Administration at Oxford University, which is where he was when I contacted HSM through the website's enquiry form to request an interview.

An HSM employee named Jazz replied that day. Her correspondence was cheery and timely, and while it occurs to me now that Jazz was probably short for Jasmine, at the time her name seemed poetic. She was Jazz not of the happy-dust, speakeasy variety, but the jazz hands of a school musical: joyous, unselfconscious, the feeling of being hangover-free on a weekend morning. I wondered if all employees of the organisation had similarly aspirational names: Star, Faith, Joy, Patience.

Jazz said it would be best to email Chris directly. I was intimidated, and coped by preparing long, sycophantic questions that he answered within a couple of weeks, apologising for his lateness and inviting me to chat with him on Skype if his responses were insufficient.

Sometime later I discovered that one of Alexander's closest friends had dated Chris's sister. Alexander and Chris had known each other. By then it seemed too much time had elapsed to Skype Chris, and I didn't know what to ask that I hadn't already. All the questions I asked people during that time were essentially variations on the same two: What happened to Alexander? How might it not have happened?

Chris's responses were thoughtful but perfunctory. Most were shorter than the questions, and one that simply read 'see above' made me realise I had elaborately asked the same thing twice. I wondered if the questions bored him, if he had given similar answers to similarly repetitive questions many times before.

I was curious about why he believed HSM had become so popular. Chris said for him and, he thought, for others, regular blogging was the reason. It made people accountable to their sobriety pledge, as well as being a means to reflect on the way they, and society, drank.

I wondered if, with so much access to their thoughts, he had any insight into why Australians drank the way they did. Chris explained that people joined HSM for four main reasons:

> 1. Confidence—the ability to stop thinking the things we have learned to think in our lifetime (e.g. I can't dance or talk to a stranger).
>
> 2. Identity—often drinking to excess becomes part of a person's identity so much so that to stop is a kind of psychological death.
>
> 3. Emotions—life is hard, alcohol softens the blow of experiencing it fully, like all drugs.
>
> 4. Purpose—people question who they are and what they want to do with their life, alcohol has been a big gap filler of experience for too many years.

To me, the ability to offer simple insights into a seemingly complex problem is one of HSM's strengths. For instance, to become a member, you must answer a series of questions about how you drink. Upon finishing the questionnaire you are shown a graph with the advised maximum drinking recommendations and how you compare, as well as a sentence-long assessment of your drinking habits. Mine was: 'Your drinking is potentially harmful to your health.'

But the reasons Chris gave were applicable to people all over the world. It didn't explain the specific drunken comportment of Australians.

Donald Horne, always an insightful thinker on such things, observed: 'To understand Australian concepts of enjoyment one must understand that in Australia there is a battle between puritanism and a kind of paganism…To drink became one of the tests of manliness among those who rejected at least some of the standards of puritanism.'

I wonder, too, if the right to drink in Australia has historically been conflated with the attainment of full citizenship. In convict Australia, once a prisoner was freed he could buy alcohol. Gender struggles were played out in public bars. With the recognition of citizenship came the lifting of prohibition for First Australians.

Maybe, in this place where Indigenous and non-Indigenous people have lived together so few years, where we are still uneasy about our identity, the Australian citizen's right to be drunk is a touchstone, a unifying element in a disparate community. It reaches across classes, races and sexes, creating a false semblance of egalitarianism. Full citizenship is the right to be drunk in whatever way it manifests—blacking out, punching someone, jumping off a bridge.

Or perhaps the collective difficulties we have with alcohol come down to our nation being young, remote and prosperous, with leisure time and lots of liquor stores, a powerful alcohol industry and wide social disparities.

When I asked Chris Raine if he really thought that organisations like HSM could change Australia's drinking culture, he responded: 'You need the political and social will to be effective.

Policy change is important in order to affect the choice architecture of people. Governments should try different levers to affect demand and supply of alcohol. These are the blunt end of cultural change—incremental, slow and universal. A social movement is the pointy end of cultural change. When society wants change and is willing to do something about it, even make a personal sacrifice to achieve it.'

Alexander's friend who dated Chris's sister told me that in 2009, Chris's first sober year and the year Alexander died, Chris went with my brother's mates to a pub called the Orient to observe their drinking behaviour. Afterwards he asked his sister and Alexander's friend to email the group from that night a link to HSM, which they did. 'A few boys posted blogs about the Orient on there…I remember having chats with Muir about it occasionally,' he wrote to me.

When I checked before I finished writing this book, Chris's sister was friends with Alexander on Facebook. Alexander doesn't have a profile or cover photo anymore, but photos and comments are still there. I scrolled through them. Most are of Alexander in various states of drunkenness, but on this occasion I noticed one I'd never really looked at before.

The photo was taken while Alexander was still at school. It's a picture of his relay swimming team. He is holding a silver trophy with a cup the size of his head, and standing next to three other boys holding a huge wooden shield. The four boys are grinning.

In the comments below one of the boys has written, 'how sweet was that win. didnt muir anchor us to victory?'

'Yer im pretty sure. Muir was the powerhouse to bring us home,' another writes.

'muir didnt breathe the entire 50 [metres] hey. gallant effort.'

It's stupid to wonder, but I indulge myself for a moment. Alexander trained in the early morning; what if his conversations about drinking that year had led to something concrete? What if he'd gone home after his exam because he was swimming the next day? Even as I write that, I know it's mad. It wouldn't have happened, because I just don't think he was in a place where he thought his drinking was a problem. I wonder if, had he been born a few years later, when movements like HSM were gaining momentum, things would have ended differently.

And then another, darker thought comes into my head, unbidden. How, how did my brother, who could swim fifty metres without breathing, drown?

It's stupid to wonder *what if?* It will drive you crazy. I close the page and shut my laptop.

19

RED FROGS

In the second week of November 2013 I drove down to Surfers Paradise. It was hot, the air-conditioning was stuffed and the car stank because the cat had pissed on the backseat. I was listening to the same fuzzy Nat King Cole tape I always listened to since it got jammed in the player. The traffic on the highway was fitful. Yellow-lit skyscrapers clustered on the edge of the black sea. As I neared town the line of cars slowed right down. Alongside Adrenalin Park—home of the Vomatron—the lights turned red. I stopped. The tape clicked over.

Until the late 1950s Surfers was small and fibro, and squatted in the dunes behind a long, angry beach. From then on developers extracted the asbestos shacks and, in the cavities, planted tall towers. Some fading pink houses still hunker in the shadows. But mostly it is hard to believe that the glass monoliths haven't always been there.

Beneath the buildings sandy one-way streets twist between small tourist operators, chicken shops, Chinese take-aways, piercing parlours, nightclubs, theatre restaurants, a wax museum, designer-clothing outlets and souvenir stores selling eucalypt-scented creams. The bright, bleak mini-metropolis draws people from all over the country looking for temperate weather, nightlife and hard bodies; sex, drugs and booze.

At this time every year new high-school graduates—those who can afford to rent an apartment here—jam into the skyscrapers and spill out onto the streets to celebrate the end of school. From mid-November to the first week of December the town is stuffed with drunken school leavers and hangers-on—opportunistic older men looking for an inexperienced drunk to fight, fuck or photograph; concerned do-gooders; and journalists gleefully documenting the melange of underage drinking and balcony hopping, unprotected sex and police arrests.

Schoolies started here at the Broadbeach Hotel in 1979. That year it was attended by a handful of Brisbane private-school graduates. In 2013 there were approximately thirty thousand school leavers on the Gold Coast, paying between five hundred and one thousand dollars to rent an apartment. Most people come for a week, and attendees are loosely staggered by state. In the first week it's primarily Queensland graduates, the second and third it's mostly New South Wales and Victorian graduates; but people come from all over the country. The three-week party leaves the

Gold Coast economy approximately sixty million dollars richer and has spawned similar events in Byron Bay, the Sunshine Coast, Stradbroke Island, The Whitsundays, Rottnest Island, Victor Harbour, Bali and Fiji.

The last time I was here at this end of the year I had just graduated, the car still smelt new and at Adrenalin Park—if you were a naked teenage girl—you could ride the Slingshot free. The Slingshot is a ride with a rotating double seat suspended by bungee ropes from two multicoloured cranes. It catapults from ground level to eighty metres above the earth at 160 kilometres per hour.

On the second last night of my 2001 stay, just before the park closed a friend of mine negotiated with the salt-pickled Slingshot operator to let us ride in our togs for a few dollars each. Cheered on by a small group of mostly older male onlookers, we took our clothes off and walked up the steps to the seat. The operator sealed us in with rollercoaster harnesses, a siren blasted and we went flying through the air.

At the end of the bungee cords' tether the seat jerked and spun the right way round, and we seemed to halt for a millisecond. Through the buildings, beyond the sand, the ocean was flat and dark to the horizon, where it poured into space. For a moment, free from school and parents, and drunk on cheap wine mixed with green cordial, it felt for me like the beginning of everything.

The seat flipped again and we fell into the yawning maw of the park, where the operator stood with his leering cronies. We disembarked from the ride to wolf-whistles and catcalls. Once we were clothed the bulk of onlookers melted into the shadows under the skyscrapers. My friend and I walked away, smirking at the ease with which we could trade our youth for stuff. Our bodies were not unthinkingly possessed—we contemplated them, bemoaned them and tried to change them—but despite their perceived imperfections they were desired, so they were a source of power. And for the first time they were entirely ours.

Schoolies is ostensibly a festival of freedom. The National Schoolies website states: 'The most enduring Schoolies Week tradition is the first run down the beach and dive into the ocean after school is finished forever. That plunge of freedom is the essence of freedom Schoolies symbolises.' To secure a unit through one of the main Schoolies websites, users click through tabs titled: 'Five steps to freedom'. The last tab redirects users to an online store featuring official Schoolies singlets and trucker caps.

The freedom Schoolies embodies is freedom from traditional disciplinarians—schoolteachers, coaches, parents, foster carers, grandparents, boarding mistresses and masters. And it is freedom of the body. There is no one dictating what to wear; what time, where and with whom to wake and sleep; what and when to eat. Most importantly, no one regulates what and how much is drunk. If freedom is the essence of Schoolies, then alcohol is the essence of that freedom. A 2010 FARE survey found that more than two-thirds of Schoolies expected to consume more than ten standard drinks per night.

The inverse reaction to bodily liberation is a growing restriction on physical freedom. Where once Broadbeach was open to everyone, now a huge area containing two dance stages is fenced off for the first week. Hurricane fences, guarded at intervals by plainclothes police, line the streets. Outside each apartment building security guards check hotel passes: Schoolies are unable to enter a hotel other than their own after 6 p.m. There's a twenty-four-hour hotline for concerned parents, and following the falling death of an attendee in 2012 some hotels now lock their balcony doors for the duration of the event.

Spinning around the edge of the teenage mass are dozens of adult satellite groups who manage and cosset the attendees. They check IDs, put on entertainment, hand out food, perform first aid, walk Schoolies home and provide emergency shelter. These people include police, emergency services, council workers, Schoolies organisers, security guards, triage workers, local businesses, chaplaincy organisations, hotel managers, and volunteers.

Arguably the largest and most successful of these groups is the hotel-chaplaincy organisation Red Frogs. Red Frogs started almost twenty years ago to provide support to school leavers at Surfers Paradise. Now it is an international organisation with a volunteer base numbering in the thousands, and a regular presence at Schoolie and Leaver weeks, University O-Weeks and music festivals, as well as high-profile sporting events like the Ashes. The group's adage is: we're not anti-drinking, we're just anti-ending-up-in-hospital.

Many of the services Red Frogs provides at and leading up to Schoolies are not radical innovations. In the months before November, Red Frogs runs a school-education program for Year Twelve students focusing on what to expect at Schoolies. The call centre that the group operates for the three weeks of Schoolies and the walk-home program where volunteers ('Froggers') are available to accompany Schoolies back to their apartments at night are services other not-for-profits and the Queensland government also provide.

The most visible difference is the group's namesake: the small red frog-shaped sweet, available from school tuckshops and convenience stores nationwide. Like grandmothers, Willy Wonka, the Easter Bunny and child snatchers, Red Frogs have hit upon a timeless and highly effective method for connecting with young people—they hand out lollies.

I met Red Frogs' founder, Andy Gourley, in the week leading up to the 2013 Schoolies. He was in the middle of a busy school-presentation schedule and had given up his lunch break to meet with me. Although I got to the appointed place on time he was already sitting at a table. He was wearing a black polo shirt with an embroidered red frog over the right breast, and his scruffy salt-and-pepper hair framed a kind round face with a short beard and moustache.

As I was sitting down Andy began to insist that he buy me food—anything I wanted. He spoke in a slow coasty drawl peppered with naff colloquialisms like *awesome*, *rad* and *dude*, and swore that the rice paper rolls at the small bookshop café where we met were the absolute best—although I felt like he might have said the same thing had we been buying lukewarm pies from a service station. It was quickly evident that the generosity which typifies Red Frogs stems from him. His ability to give—food, compliments, time, attention—is seemingly effortless, involuntary and compulsive.

Andy started Red Frogs almost accidentally in 1995. At university he became involved with Citipointe, a Pentecostal mega-church in an outer Brisbane suburb run by an attractive-looking husband-and-wife team. Through the church he started doing youth work. For a few years he'd been working with a group of high-school students, and every Friday night he took them skateboarding. They would bomb car parks, run away from security guards and hang out until the early morning. Their parents didn't really care. When the students went to Schoolies they invited Andy to visit—only the security guard wouldn't allow him to enter the hotel where they were staying, because he didn't have a pass.

He said to the guard, 'Mate, I'm their youth worker. I know what they're doing in your building and I can be far more benefit up there than I can down here,' but it didn't work. So Andy went to the hotel manager and asked: 'Do you want a hand with this?' To which she replied, 'How much?' and he said, 'Free—I'll come down and lend a hand with some of my church mates.' The manager decided to give him a try.

It started in that hotel. Andy and his friends would go from room to room wearing shirts screenprinted with the words HOTEL CHAPLAINCY NETWORK. 'We just started crashing parties, going floor to floor—finding dudes passed out on stairwells, hanging over verandahs and down on beaches; we'd pick them up from down there.'

But they were having trouble convincing people to let them into the rooms—it would take about ten minutes before kids felt comfortable enough to open the door fully. So Andy asked his friend Luke to go down to the corner store beneath the hotel and buy all its stock of red frogs.

When they brought the lollies back for the first time, the kids in the hotel room went berserk. Some called their friends and yelled down the phone that they had red frogs. Other Schoolies started coming from different floors to get a share of the bounty. Andy looked at the sweets and thought: 'This is awesome.' That year the Hotel Chaplaincy Organisation bought all the red frogs for sale on the Gold Coast and, soon after, other hotels started contacting them.

As the organisation grew, so did its services. As well as the Red Frogs hotline, which took 10,835 calls in 2012; walk-homes; and the school-presentation series, which is seen by forty thousand Year Twelve students, Red Frogs runs seven entertainment stages, including one at the Gold Coast Schoolies; cooks pancakes by request in apartments; and even assists in cleaning up units when Schoolies leave. In 2013 Allen's donated sixteen tonnes of Red Frogs to the organisation.

I asked Andy if he thought Red Frogs was taking responsibility away from Schoolies. If people can party without the usual consequences, isn't the organisation just creating a more comfortable environment for the same problems to perpetuate?

'There are two schools of thought,' he said. The first is that the Schoolies should learn from their mistakes. 'But then you have to ask yourself if you're comfortable walking past someone drowning in their own vomit or getting raped on the beach.' The second is that, by being a positive part of the culture, Red Frogs is creating off-ramps for people to opt out in a positive way. By providing non-drinkers with a role—the designated sober person—they're allowing them to be comfortable as a sober person with their drinking friends.

'But is it working?' I asked.

'Schoolies has changed a lot. Kids are bringing decent food down, they're drinking lots of water, they're going to bed early and I haven't had a bottle thrown at my car for two years.' He described it as like being a fence at the top of a cliff. 'We're stopping people from falling off.'

After lunch Andy invited me to come down to Schoolies the following week. As well as looking after Schoolies, Red Frogs runs tours for media, corporate sponsors and miscellaneous extras like me.

—

The traffic lights next to Adrenalin Park changed and the column of cars slid forward. I turned off the main highway into an underground garage. I walked out, emerging on a thin strip of footpath. The street, dissected by road works, was a cold pottage of bitumen and dirt entrails. In front of me the pavement was viscous with seventeen-year-olds. They were wild, joyous, beautiful, selfish, and the town was so obviously theirs I felt apologetic as I squeezed past.

I walked through a strip mall to get to the hotel where I was supposed to meet Larnie, Andy's personal assistant. I was running late and when I arrived in the hotel foyer there was no one around, except for a few luckless grey-haired tourists on couches. I asked the man at the reception counter if Larnie had left a message and he shrugged, shaking his head. 'Try upstairs,' he said, pointing to the large curved staircase in the centre of the room.

About halfway up the stairs I saw a trestle table with a Red Frogs banner. There were two young guys sitting behind it. At the top I could see behind the railing, and I stared at the large group of twenty-somethings in black Red Frogs T-shirts. They were sitting and lying on the floor, listening to music, chatting and yawning, and they were sober. It was early—about 7 p.m.—so I thought that they must be waiting until later to walk the streets.

'I'm here to see Larnie,' I told the boy at the trestle table. He smiled—an easy, open smile. All the volunteers I met were young and friendly. I found this strange, because I expected them to be sanctimonious, cynical and tired, or obviously evangelical. I checked them surreptitiously for some kind of stereotypical sign—a cross, a headscarf, orthopaedic shoes, shapeless clothing, sensible haircuts—but the only unifying trait of the volunteers I met was that they were really nice, almost eerily so.

To volunteer with Red Frogs for a week at Schoolies costs between $50 and $330. This will buy five to seven sleepless nights either deciphering drunken garble over the phone or accompanying inebriated Schoolies back to their buildings. It will give volunteers the chance to cook food for, and clean the apartments of, hungover graduates probably on their first unsupervised trip away from home. It might even purchase an opportunity to fish someone out of a spa bath or wipe up their shit. And yet, the year before I went down, there were more than seven hundred volunteers for the Gold Coast Schoolies alone, a few of whom were back for their tenth year.

Most Red Frog volunteers are in their early twenties. Some volunteer because it's a way to give back. They've already, as Andy told me, 'been there, done that and had the peas-and-carrots shirt'. For others it's a way to be part of the party without having to partake in the drinking. Red Frog volunteers get treated like 'rock stars'.

'It's an honour, hey,' Andy told me. 'To be there literally saving people is amazing. It's a real privilege, and you get a real sense of fulfilment out of helping here. These are crew who really do love helping people. They love it.' It's like aid work, only they're looking after drunk teenagers.

Andy told me about a girl who was sitting in a spa bath, so drunk she didn't realise or care that she was slipping underwater, and someone came in and grabbed her just in time. He told me about cooking one morning in someone's hotel room when water started coming out from under the bathroom door and pooling around their feet. He went in and found 'old mate' passed out with his bum on the plughole, so they woke him up and stopped him from drowning.

He told me about a crew of Red Frogs who found a girl passed out with vomit and shit all over her. They put her in the shower, changed her clothes and put her in bed. Then they cleaned up the apartment. When her friends got home they had no idea of the state she'd been in.

In passing, I mentioned this last story to one of my former housemates. I thought it was sort of heroic, but she was disturbed. 'You mean they took her clothes off while she was passed out?'

My former housemate is a support worker in a women's shelter. A lot of the women who access the shelter have been sexually abused. 'I would never touch a woman without her permission, let alone undress her. That's really not okay,' she said. 'Who was cleaning her? Was it another woman or a man? And how did they even find her in there?'

'I don't know,' I said. 'Maybe she called them before she passed out.'

'How do they know nothing is happening between the volunteers and the Schoolies in the apartments? They're young, drunk teenagers, and young, sober strangers in positions of trust are going into their units.'

Red Frog volunteers must already be from a pastoral organisation or church, and a lot of them come through organisations similar to Red Frogs. Andy said that Red Frogs recruits organisations rather than individuals, because 'it only takes one idiot to blow us out of the water, to do the wrong thing, then you're toast.' Volunteers get their own organisational check before they arrive at Red Frogs; all volunteers must have a Blue Card for working with children; and Red Frogs has a system of checking a volunteer's credibility, as well.

I said all this to my former housemate. She looked at me hard. 'So the fact that they come through a church organisation is going to stop something happening? Don't be silly.'

I thought on this briefly as I walked with the boy from the Red Frogs information desk over to a group of people talking at the back of the room. While there are other organisations founded in Queensland to help combat the problems caused by alcohol abuse, all of which have had a degree of success, Red Frogs is the only one that has such a huge physical reach. It has managed to grow a credible presence at many of the biggest drinking events around the country. Despite the potential for pitfalls—and there has been none that I know of so far—shouldn't that be encouraged?

When we got to the group a man with facial hair introduced himself as Brendan and the tall, thin South African man standing next to him as Craig. Larnie, a short and predictably friendly woman with brown hair, appeared soon after. There were two other people on the tour with me—an app developer and the owner of a roofing company whose employee volunteered with the organisation. Larnie issued us each with Friends of Red Frogs shirts, black shoulder bags and a kilo bag of the eponymous lollies. She told us to get changed into our shirts but emphasised that we had to return them. 'We have to be really careful with those shirts because they look so similar to the volunteer shirts. Even though we know you wouldn't try, you might be able to get access to a hotel room wearing one, so we need them back.'

The first stop on our tour was the phone room. About ten people of various ages sat looking at computer screens. They had headsets on and they were taking calls from Schoolies all over Australia. There was a television on the end wall with a bar graph tallying the types of calls the centre was receiving: walk-homes, random acts of pancakes, and other. The graph was live. It updated every time a call-centre volunteer entered information about the reason for their call.

Amusing calls were written up on Post-it notes and pinned to the wall outside the call centre for other Red Frog volunteers to read. The Post-it notes said things like:

Them: Hey, can we get a team out?

Me: What for?

Them: My mate is drunk and he's stuck in a doorway.

Schoolie: Can I please get a walk-home?

Me: Where are you?

Schoolie: Oh, sorry. I've just been told I'm in the foyer of my hotel.

After we inspected the internal operations we went out onto the street. We walked around the corner of the hotel; a young woman was sitting on a plastic chair, vomiting onto the pavement. Two Red Frog volunteers stood with her: one held back her hair while another—a Frogger no older than the Schoolies—saw us and called for help.

Brendan and Craig went over. While we were waiting I asked Larnie if there was a method for handing out the frogs. She told me it was a good idea to push a few up to the top of the bag and create a type of cone for them to sit in by gripping its neck. This was in case a Schoolie tried to put his or her hand right in and grab a fistful.

It reminded me of feeding kangaroos at Lone Pine Sanctuary when I was a kid. You had to pour a small quantity of pellets onto your right palm and hold the brown paper bag with the rest of the pellets behind your back. Otherwise the kangaroos would try to eat what was in the brown paper bag, instead of taking what you offered.

When Brendan and Craig had seen to the vomiting girl we restarted our tour. About five minutes in, three boys stopped us outside a nightclub and asked if they could have lollies. Larnie gestured to me, so I pushed some frogs to the top of the bag, squeezing the neck tightly. There were two each. 'Here you are,' I said, proffering my stingy fare. The boys picked them up between forefinger and thumb and said thank you. Their unexpected politeness was disarming and slightly disappointing. I had expected them to be more ravenous.

Brendan, Craig and Larnie took us down Cavill Avenue. It was a mess of kids. Now and then one of them asked us if we knew where a toilet was, but we were mostly left alone. Another man on the tour turned to me and said, 'Why do they need to drink so much?' I shrugged and mumbled something. We continued to the beach. It was very different from when I was here last. While it was important then, it was now the focal point of Schoolies. A huge area was cordoned off with temporary hurricane fencing. Schoolies lined up to enter it. Beside one of the entrances was the Red Frogs walk-home tent. There was no one there at that moment, but we were told it had been busy all night.

We followed Brendan through a gap in the hurricane fence and emerged at the back of the Red Frogs entertainment stage. There was a camera crew backstage, so we waited outside for a moment. A small, pretty girl with shiny hair came over to us and walked along the row introducing herself. She knew our names already. We followed her up the back stairs of the tent and stood on the side of the stage looking out. In the foreground were three or four Red Frogs volunteers dancing manically, while beyond them the crowd pressed up against the fence with hands outstretched, screaming and jiggling.

The small, pretty girl was going nuts beside me. 'Do you want to come dance up the front of the stage?' she asked. I pursed my lips and shook my head. 'No, thank you.' No one else did either. This was apparently unusual. The girl told me that the people who came on the tour—the CEOs of sponsor organisations and media representatives—usually took them up on the offer. 'They go crazy,' she told me.

A few minutes later the DJ looked at us and mouthed something over the music. 'He's asking if anyone wants to press the button for the next song,' Larnie said. They seemed eager for us to take part in proceedings, so I volunteered. I walked over to the booth and the two DJs parted, allowing me to stand between them. 'You'll have to press the silver button—we'll count you in.'

All three of us were standing there staring at it. I was stationary. The other two were bouncing, each with one hand on a headphone. They counted me in and I pressed the button. I watched the crowd but there seemed to be no change. 'Thanks,' the DJ said. 'You want to cue another song?'

The Red Frogs dancers seemed to be high on life. Their manic gyrating was arresting; as a reserved dancer, I found it difficult to look away. I was a little embarrassed by their exuberance. They, however, were not at all embarrassed. They looked overjoyed to be there, throwing out water bottles, doing shout-outs, falling onto their knees then popping back up again. The stage transcended the party-crashing tactics of the Red Frogs teams. Here, the Schoolies came to them.

Andy told me later that they used specific tactics to control the crowd. As the night wore on they began to play dull songs so the kids would run to the stage at the other end of the enclosure. The other stage followed suit, and the Schoolies ran up and down the beach until they were all tuckered out and went home.

We were ushered out of the dance tent a few minutes after I pressed the silver button. Brendan took us to the triage tent, where sick Schoolies came for assistance and the drunkest ones stayed the night. Larnie told me that it was important for Schoolies not to pass out in the dunes, because that's where people got attacked, and in the morning a sand sweeper made the beach smooth, indiscriminately pushing debris to the side—aluminium cans, straws, glass bottles, thongs and immobile seventeen-year-olds. I thought perhaps she was exaggerating but I hadn't seen a sand sweeper before.

The last stop on the trip was Andy's apartment. He didn't stay at the Red Frogs' hotel because he was working almost all the time and needed some time alone. When we entered his apartment there was a small crowd cooking, eating and sitting around chatting. Like all the volunteers I had met they were warm, open, quick to smile, and young. We made our way onto the balcony, past a display of soft drinks.

On the left side of the balcony was a table covered in fruit, biscuits, cheese and small canapés. Andy was talking to a group of people who I thought might be journalists. He went from person to person making introductions, making sure no one was alone, making sure everyone had something to eat. He listened with interest; he remembered who we were and why we were there.

There was something about his scruffy hair and beard, small potbelly and board shorts that was endearing and approachable. It belied the fact that this enormous, tightly run organisation, which operates under difficult circumstances, came from his head. People come back, year after year, because of what he created.

I looked over the edge. Far beneath us was the beach enclosure. At the entrance hundreds of Schoolies were lining up to get in and, next to it, hundreds more were streaming out the exit. We were closest to the Schoolies.com stage, but up the other end of the enclosure Schoolies stood hundreds thick outside the Red Frogs stage. For the first time the vast scale of the event was apparent to me. So too was the enormousness of the Red Frogs operation, at least at this event—which I suppose was the point of the final tour stop.

Brendan and the app designer were standing next to me. 'It's beautiful up here,' I said. And it was. At that height, the buildings that exacerbated the scruffy chaos on the streets provided sanctuary from it. The surrounding skyscrapers seemed more manageable and their shapes were easier to make out. They twisted and arced towards the ozone, smooth and stained with lit windows.

'I like being up here in a storm,' Brendan said. He pointed at a long pole at the top of another building. 'The lightning hits that conductor and it's amazing.' We were quiet for a moment as we looked out. It was the first time in the night that Brendan had shared something of himself and not been a Red Frog volunteer. Then someone brought over a platter of hot arancini balls, the app developer walked off, the noise from the beach became noticeable again and Brendan turned to speak to someone else.

Andy came over to see if I was okay. 'Have you eaten?' he asked.

'Yes,' I mumbled through my mouthful and held up half an arancini ball.

'They're great, aren't they? One of the Froggers makes them. He's studying to be a chef. He's a genius in the kitchen.' We looked over the balcony. 'How many people do you think are over at the Red Frogs stage?' he asked.

'I don't know,' I replied. 'There seem to be a few.'

'It's a bit hard to tell from here. But it looks pretty good.' He pointed to the beach and some people standing in the waves. 'That's where they go to the toilet.'

'That's probably where I would go too,' I said. 'If I were busting.'

There was a brief pause. 'Down there are the future doctors, lawyers and CEOs,' Andy said.

This was a line I had heard earlier in the evening. These seemed to be the three most worthwhile professions to the Red Frogs, or the three that had the most marketing impact when explaining why the organisation was important. 'We make sure the future doctors, lawyers and CEOs make it through their irresponsible years,' they might have said.

I looked at the people pissing in the ocean, then over at the Red Frogs volunteers in the kitchen. Some were helping the chef plate up arancini balls. Others were handing around food. Some were standing around talking and laughing. They all had full control of their fine-motor skills. They all seemed to be having a good time.

Actually, it seems as if the future leaders are up here, I thought.

We left Andy's apartment. Larnie stayed behind: she and the Red Frogs volunteers said goodbye. We took the lift back down to the street, then started walking briskly back to the hotel where the Red Frogs were based. On the way we walked past someone slumped against the wall. Craig and Brendan started to help him up. His head lolled around against his chest. When they got him to his feet he could barely walk, so they put him in between them and wrapped his arms around their shoulders. They shuffled a few metres, then he seemed to revive. He shrugged them off, stood up and staggered off. Craig and Brendan walked back to the group. We strode off again.

A hundred metres from the hotel a boy stopped us and asked for a frog. 'Here,' I said and passed him the bag.

When he was gone the app developer looked at me. 'You're not supposed to give them out here,' he said. 'If he dropped it, it would get stuck to the pavement. The council doesn't like it.'

Brendan turned and said it was fine, just this once. He seemed tired.

Back at the hotel I took off my Red Frogs T-shirt in the bathroom and put my regular shirt back on. When I returned to the meeting point there was no one there but another attractive blond woman. I gave her the T-shirt, and asked if she could tell Craig and Brendan that I said goodbye.

'Did you like your trip?' she asked.

'Yes,' I replied.

'Thank you *so much* for coming,' she said.

—

A few months later I was at a party and I mentioned that I was writing about the Red Frogs. The girl I was talking to said, 'Oh, I remember them from Schoolies. They kidnapped me.' I asked her to tell me more and she said, 'I was with a group of friends going to a beach party. None of us were very drunk but on the way we met another group of girls who were really drunk, so we were helping them. Anyway, just after we met up with them, a Red Frog came up and asked where we were going. We said we were going to the beach party, and the Red Frog convinced us it was lame and that we should go to another party nearby. We followed because we were seventeen and, you know, you still did what people told you to then.

'When we got there it was all right. There was a band playing and people were dancing, so we did too, but then one of my friends came up to me and said, "Have you listened to the lyrics?" It was Christian rock. It wasn't really my kind of thing, so we went to leave, but we were told to wait because there was a surprise coming.

'The band stopped playing and a man came out. He asked us all to sit down, then he started telling us how he found Jesus. He said—and I think of this every time I'm driving—that it happened after his wife had a car accident and her shins splintered up into her knees.

'He talked for a little while longer, then he asked who of us now accepted Jesus into our lives. Some people put their hands up, so he let them go. He wouldn't let us leave until we'd put our hands up.'

'Did you?' I asked.

'I had to.'

None of the Red Frogs I had met talked about God except Andy, but only because I asked him about it. When I asked if any of the Schoolies are put off by a religious organisation he said: 'Not really—it's a really non-confrontational program; it's not preachy at all. So if guys want to chat, they can—but otherwise you're pretty much cleaning up vomit most of the time and walking dudes home and stuff like that.'

In the 2009 book *Jesus Loves You... This I Know* the authors, Craig Gross and Jason Harper, describe spending a week with the Red Frogs. They write about how the Red Frogs organisers would tell the volunteers over and over, 'Find your one person you made your connection with and key in on that. Go back to that hotel room and follow up on that.' The authors describe the success of three Red Frogs volunteers who turn up at Citipointe church the week after Schoolies, bleary-eyed but each with a Schoolie in tow. 'You see,' one of the authors wrote, 'each of them had found their one. A smile spread across my face so large when I heard that the three Schoolies who these Frogs had poured into the whole week had decided to come to church.'

I asked the girl at the party what she thought about having to accept Jesus before she could leave the room. 'I don't know,' she replied. 'Now, I think it's pretty bad. But back then I was seventeen; I still did what I was told. I guess I've mostly always thought it was kind of funny. But I was really pissed I missed the beach party.'

20
CRAB SHELL

I flew to Melbourne in August 2015. In Brisbane it was spring weather; in Melbourne it was six degrees and raining.

It was past midnight when I arrived and caught a cab to the house of a friend I'd once lived with. It was on the edge of Victoria Park, in Abbotsford—a low-set brick bungalow, with a gated front door and dark trees in the front garden. Inside were cupboards, everywhere—up high, down low, where fireplaces used to be—and on on the outside of the some of the room doors there was more than one bolt. When my friend, Kylie, moved in she told me that her partner, Craig, said, 'It looked like a group of war criminals had built it and were still living in the roof.' Then she laughed and kind of sobbed at the same time.

No one answered when I knocked, so I let myself in and walked down the hallway. At the end was a door. It opened onto a yellow-lit living room where Kylie and Craig sat at a table covered in chocolate: chocolate melts, chocolate-covered coffee beans and half a chocolate cake with a giraffe centrepiece. The giraffe was wearing a Carmen Miranda icing hat. Its skirt was festooned with coloured jubes.

They yelled with delight when they saw me, and I wanted to cry. Over the course of writing this book I had broken up with two boyfriends, a girlfriend, a best friend. I had fought with my housemate, workmates, parents. My friends had grown up, found jobs, moved in with partners, married, given birth, and I had watched them enviously, bitterly, mired in self-pity. From my despondent eddy, it seemed everyone else had floated on. I was furious and envious, and as I grew more furious I treated old, good friends with destructive abandon.

I sat down on a padded chair in the yellow living room feeling like a grub in compost. Kylie poured me an espresso martini. The empty vessel was replaced by Prosecco in an old-fashioned champagne glass. At the base of the bowl was a blob of colour: a nipple, generous and misshapen. Another glass appeared, and another. When that went, there was smoky, peaty whisky, with ice. On the bottle was a galley in full sail against a stormy sky. 'This is delicious,' I said, and held my glass out for more.

The metamorphosis from soft grub to brown-backed beetle was swift and wonderful. In my head I composed what I assumed were difficult-to-resist emails to a one-time lover I had never quite got over, while witticisms fell from my mouth.

At 4.30 a.m. I crawled into bed with my clothes on. I know it was 4.30 because a few days later, when I happened to check my sent-email folder, I saw a one-line message I had sent the one-time lover. At the end of the single sentence was a string of emojis with no discernible connection: a rocket, an embarrassed face, a worm, a heart and a pistol.

At midday I woke in a fug. My beetle flesh was leached of fluid, although the carapace was still thick. Kylie and Craig were in the kitchen. 'Can I show you our caravan kitchen?' Kylie asked. 'This is the fold-up inbuilt plastic chopping board,' she said, and lifted a large portion of the bench. 'Whisky with your coffee?'

'I think I have to go back to bed for half an hour,' I said, and went to the toilet to vomit.

In my room I tried to sleep. Craig sent me a message telling me there was coffee and aspirin outside the door. I crawled to the entrance and on top of a pretty tray were a china cup and two tiny porcelain bowls holding two pills each. I drank the coffee and felt nauseated. I thought it would be impolite of me to vomit too many times in the bathroom, so I emptied one side of my toiletries bag, and vomited in there instead. Over time, as the bile went cold and seeped up through the fabric, that side became clammy, so I emptied the other side and kept going. It was a good feeling: primal, relieving. I rested the bag of coffee-scented stomach fluids against my overnight bag and got dressed.

That evening, I met my old housemate Anna at her place. She made me a Campari with soda, and I perched on the side of the bath and talked to her as she brushed on thick black eye shadow. On the way out she put a bottle of wine in my bag, like we had done in our early twenties, and we went to a Thai restaurant for dinner.

We ordered a papaya and salt-crab salad. When the salad arrived, instead of flesh the papaya was mixed with sharp, empty pieces of exoskeleton.

'Are we supposed to eat the flesh out of these?' Anna held a small black cylinder in the air—part of a leg, maybe.

I had ordered the salad, and felt defensive. 'Mm, there is no flesh in those. That must just be how they make it here.'

'I've never had a papaya salad before, but this is disgusting,' she said, and picked at the curry instead.

I ate defiantly. A piece of leg caught on a ridge at the roof of my mouth. I fished it out. 'You're right. It is.'

Afterwards, we walked to The Tote. In the dark upstairs bar Anna found two water glasses and we used them for the warm wine in my bag. A slight, blue-haired woman in a leopard-print tube dress told me she liked my outfit. 'It's really cute—you look like you're about to go horse riding.' I stood in front of the smoke machine watching the writhing bodies, and trying to drink enough wine that I wouldn't feel like a large perverted jockey in the mist.

Anna's new boyfriend was the DJ. When he finished his set she introduced me to him. 'This is my best friend,' she said. 'She's writing a book.'

He was wearing a suit that had sharp, smooth lapels. His collar was toothpaste-white and rigid with starch. 'What's it about?' he asked.

'The drinking culture,' I said, gesturing apologetically with my glass.

'Well, you've come to the right place. You'll find some of the biggest lushes in Australia in this bar.' He smiled proudly.

'What's a lush?' Anna asked.

'It's someone who drinks a lot. It's an old-fashioned term.' He paused, then swivelled neatly into a group of men discussing football.

'He loves AFL,' Anna explained.

Shortly after, she was subsumed into the smoke and lovely women. I was left leaning on the bar trying to look nonchalant, but I felt old, sad and shabby. An organ somewhere in my torso ached. I pushed through the slow-grinding bodies to the front of the stage, where Anna was dancing and laughing with a rapt, rotating audience. 'I'm going,' I said.

'No, stay,' she replied, and she meant it, and I loved her for it, but I felt far away from her. Once we had been inseparable; now our friendship fed off memories. 'We're doing what we both wanted to do when we were young and hungry,' she sometimes exclaimed, and I would nod, feeling shy. My life seemed to have shrunk; there were fewer people, fewer places—and I was fixated by what had gone wrong. Hers, though, had grown. She was part of a scene we once thought impenetrable, playing in bands around the city, living where she wanted to live. She was busy and she seemed mostly happy.

'I'm sorry, Anna—I can't. I'm so tired.'

She walked me out. At the door she greeted the security guard by name. 'This is my best friend,' she said, introducing me. I smiled, then turned to her and hugged her hard. 'I love you, Els,' she said.

'I love you, too,' I said, and got a cab on the corner.

Eight years earlier, from the same spot, my friend Laura and I had hitched a lift home with a newspaper editor who had been living in Jerusalem or Saudi Arabia or Indonesia. I sat in the front seat of his new four-wheel-drive and Laura, sitting in the back, said: 'Elspeth wants to be a writer.' He gave me his card and told me to call him. 'We can meet up,' he said.

A few days later I messaged him. 'I can't meet with you, I'm busy, I'm sorry,' he replied, and I wondered what compulsion had caused him to pick us up and give me his card, and what adult considerations had caused him to back out of meeting with me. After that encounter, I imagined ageing as a lap band slowly constricting life until there were very few experiences you could consume and your world thinned right down. Alcohol was an integral part of that. I thought that once you came to the point where you were sober enough to drive on a Saturday night, life must be unbearably boring.

The night we had hopped in the car, the Tote corner had felt huge; the world seemed full of obstacles and possibilities. Now it seemed smaller and grubbier. I had enough money for a cab; there was no need to hitch.

The next evening, my last evening in Melbourne, Kylie, Craig and I walked down a laneway near midnight and stopped at an unmarked door. 'This is it,' Kylie said, and pushed the handle. The door opened up to a room of dark wood, low couches and soft light. A bar ran the length of the back wall, and behind it shelves of glinting multicoloured spirits reached from chest height to the ceiling. We sat at a high table and flicked through impressively detailed cocktail menus two centimetres thick.

I ordered a whisky drink first. It had a swirl of orange rind, and was cooled with an ice chunk as round and large as a golf ball. Our second round of cocktails came with scented vapour trapped in bell jars. First you inhaled the vapour, then you drank the cocktail. The cocktails were expensive and delicious. They took a long time to prepare and were served with theatrical flare. 'Let's get another,' I begged when last drinks were called around 1 a.m. 'I'll buy them.'

The next day I woke up two hours before I was due to catch my flight. I ate half a piece of dry toast and attempted to sip on coffee. I showered, pulled on a white shirt with a grimy collar, packed my bag and hugged Craig goodbye. 'Don't vomit in the air,' he called after me. I laughed. 'I've given worse advice than that,' he said, and pulled the door shut.

On the way to the tram I threw my stained, stinking toiletries bag in a bin and felt sad. What am I doing? I wondered.

On the plane I sat across the aisle from a woman with cropped blond hair and a thick Australian accent; she looked to be in her forties. We were both seated in the front row of a budget airline—the crew had reseated the woman and her partner because the woman had an acute fear of take-off and landing. 'I'm anxious for a week before I have to fly,' I heard her tell a flight attendant. 'But this is all right, hey? This is fine. I feel fine.'

'I love flying,' the flight attendant said. 'You will, too. You're doing very well.'

'This is amazing,' the woman replied.

We began our descent. 'This is incredible—I've never looked

out the window before—look, this is incredible.' Her voice was loud and fast. There was a noise from the undercarriage. 'What was that?' the woman said. She grabbed her armrest. Infected by her fear, I gripped my own.

'It's fine,' the attendant said. 'If you don't hear anything, that's when you know we're in trouble.'

The woman relaxed. 'Usually I'd have my eyes shut—I'd be crying right now. But this is okay. This is actually grouse.'

Years before, I had watched a man see the ocean for the first time. It was early—around 6 a.m.—and I was in a small Argentinean town with a long pier and a grubby beach. The man was standing on the mineral sand, his arms outstretched, yelling with delight. His friend came up to me to explain: '*Él está viendo el mar por primera vez. Nunca lo había visto antes! Nunca!*' The man on the beach was middle-aged. He was wearing black sneakers and tracksuit pants with a navy windbreaker. I shook my head, '*Bien*,' I said, because I didn't know how to say much else in Spanish. '*Muy bien*.'

How simple it was to see something for the first time—as slight as opening your eyes when before you had kept them closed, or buying a ten-dollar bus ticket from a landlocked town to the coast—and yet how huge. The woman on the plane would fly again, and she would keep her head up for a second, third and fourth time. The man on the beach would return to the place where he lived, but it would be smaller, less significant, and the world so much bigger. He had given it context.

When I got home from the airport it was early evening and, as I often did, I walked to the Kangaroo Point end of the Story

Bridge. At the spot where the path passed a huge cream pylon splashed yellow by caged spotlights I stopped. The pylon was in a park gloomy with squat Moreton Bay figs and utilitarian barbecue huts. On the other side of the path, before the river, a brown beach curled around a dark mangrove forest. The forest might have been prehistoric, except for the chalky plastic kayak perishing in its roots.

The multicoloured lights of the bridge reflected in the opaque water made the river marble with colour. Despite the lights, the structure had a lonely heft. The underside was tracked with steel girders and the void between pylons, between the river and the road, was a vacuum.

I looked up. I didn't know which side Alexander had jumped from and had never asked. What, in the end, did I know about my youngest brother? We had lived so long apart.

A night at a music festival. My brother appeared from nowhere: 'Hello, El.'

'Hello, moo-moo.' My heart soared, as it always did when I saw his lopsided grin. I felt the visceral compulsion I'd had since he was a baby, to pull him into a crushing hug and hold his hand and keep him near me and look at his crude beauty—but I left my arms by my side.

'Are you having fun?' I asked.

'Yeah! It's awesome.' Then maybe he poked my arm a few times, making raspberry sounds. 'Okay, I'm going.'

'Where?' But he'd already loped off.

Later, I saw him alone, drunk and dancing. He was holding a beer and grinning. The stage was at the back of a paddock, and he was at the back of the crowd. Behind him were tall, thin ghost gums, above them a partial moon.

Once, when I was a kid, I stood at the door to his bedroom and asked him, 'What do you think about?' I had been in my room listening through the plasterboard wall to him chatting to himself.

'I don't know,' he said.

'What were you talking about just then?'

'I don't remember. Nothing.'

But he did know—he must have.

I looked at him dancing, and wondered the same thing.

I started writing this book in an idealistic fugue. My brother had died because alcohol addled his brain to the point where he was no longer able to make rational decisions. Had he not been drunk that night, he would probably still be alive now. The reason he consistently drank so much was because he was part of a permissive society which, rather than condemning huge drinkers and dangerous drinking behaviours, encouraged them, celebrated them. I wanted society to change so that no one else would die like Alexander; therefore, I reasoned, I too would change.

Three years after I began writing, the night before Father's Day, I went to a party and imbibed enough whisky to keep me drunk until the following evening. The morning after the party Patrick and his wife picked me up for breakfast at our parents' house. I had organised the breakfast, but when we got there all I could manage was a hug, then I crawled into my parents' bed and fell asleep. A few hours later Mum woke me up and drove me home. 'I'm sorry,' I said.

'It was your father's breakfast, not mine,' she replied.

I vomited all day. In the evening I called Dad. 'I'm sorry—I don't know what's wrong with me.'

When I was growing up my father would get angry at little things—a towel left on the bathroom floor, bad table manners, an unclean room—but he had a reservoir of calm reserved for moments where we had really messed up.

'Els, I was like you for a long time. At some point you realise you have to stop drinking like that,' he said.

How simple it was to see something, and for that something to change you. How simple, but how difficult and rare. How many imaginary crashes had the woman on the plane endured before she opened her eyes to escape them? How many times had the man postponed his bus trip before he bought the ticket to the grubby little beach that morning? I was perpetually ashamed of thinking about doing something and not having the strength of character to follow through. I thought that perhaps if I banged my head against the realisation long enough my actions would follow suit, but instead I became filled with self-loathing, unsure about anything.

Then one morning, not so long ago, an old housemate said, 'You reduce everything to a story, and in your stories events and characters are entirely one way or another. Life isn't like that. Situations aren't straightforward—there are nuances.'

She was right: I avoided thinking about grey areas. It was so much easier if there was a villain and a hero, a right way and a wrong way. Then people, situations, objects and events could be analysed and categorised and not dealt with again, except in the context of the label they had been assigned. In this way I could easily apportion blame.

My inability to stop binge drinking completely, when I knew it was the cause of Alexander's death and often the source of my own troubles, was, in my straightforward cataloguing strategy, proof that I was a shitty person. Perhaps that was in some ways true—I had always found it difficult to commit to my professed beliefs, to follow through with action, to avoid hypocrisy. But then, perhaps it also wasn't true. Like most people, I meant well, and I messed up. I knew what the right thing to do was, and sometimes I did it, and sometimes I didn't.

Alcohol is probably the most human of all mind-altering substances. It is the catalyst for so many states of being. It is a germ killer and a poison; an unremarkable but integral addition to meals and a beverage reserved to mark special events; able to enhance social occasions and destroy them; best consumed in moderation, but symbolic of excess. The ability of a person to consume it regularly in great quantities is both the sign of a strong constitution and a symptom of illness; to be in possession of particular brands of alcohol can signify wealth or poverty. Alcohol's effects are lauded in sports people, politicians and other high-profile members of society, who are often forgiven for their indiscretions while under the influence, but are considered problematic in minority groups, young people and women, who are blamed for its mismanagement.

Depending on my sober mood, alcohol can make me angry, nasty and weepy; or braver and funnier, more audacious and loving. Like a tapestry hook it pulls to the surface the threads of who you are at any particular point in time.

I knew this, and I didn't want to know this. To accept nuance was also to accept the possibility that Alexander's death could not be contained by the neat tale we had given it—a happy young man who was also a daredevil when drunk. What if, all this time, I'd been picking pieces of crab shell from my mouth and refusing to acknowledge something wasn't right? I used alcohol to be brave enough to live in the world; maybe Alexander needed it to leave.

I came across a passage in a 1913 memoir by the American novelist Jack London. It was about the author as a young man who, at the end of a long drinking spree, in a fit of liquor-induced depression, tried to commit suicide by drowning. At the conclusion of the passage is this rumination:

> And in passing, let me note that this maniacal trick John Barleycorn [drink] played me is nothing uncommon. An absolute statistic of the percentage of suicides due to John Barleycorn would be appalling. In my case, healthy, normal, young, full of the joy of life, the suggestion to kill myself was unusual; but it must be taken into account that it came on the heels of a long carouse, when my nerves and brain were fearfully poisoned, and that the dramatic, romantic side of my imagination, drink-maddened to lunacy, was delighted with the suggestion.

The possibility that Alexander committed suicide was the one thing those who knew him assiduously avoided thinking about, discussing, or believing; and, in our avoidance, in the way we tiptoed around the topic, maybe we gave it shape.

In an exercise book we found in Alexander's room after he died, there was a line or two about beer. The book disappeared soon after we discovered it—maybe a well-meaning friend wanted to spare my mother any permutations of thought about the cause of Alexander's death—but from memory the line was, in his little-boy scrawl: 'Drinking heavy beer makes me depressed, but I do it anyway.' We all saw it, but we didn't really talk about it.

It was impossible to address, because it was devastating to think that we might have missed a sign that he was not okay, that somewhere in his unfathomable thoughts were those that might cause him to want to end his own life prematurely. And that they were gestating when he was talking to himself in his bedroom and when he was dancing under the ghost gums with a beer. It was devastating, because what could have caused it? He had everything—people who loved him, somewhere to live, things he loved doing, future plans. And what if we had been able to do something about it?

Maybe that was just the way alcohol toyed with him; those depressive emotions were what the tapestry needle pulled out. Perhaps what could have prevented his death was beyond what his friends and family were able to provide.

21
THE BRIDGE

When I was in my early twenties my friend Libby, who worked for a funeral home, told me about a specific section of the Brisbane River where the bodies of people who had jumped off the Story Bridge washed up. 'The police know to go there,' she said.

At the time I thought she must have been exaggerating. I couldn't believe there were so many jumpers that the place in which their corpses surfaced might be pinpointed. In fact, between 1995 and 2007, there was roughly one jumping death from the Story Bridge every fifteen weeks.

In December 2015 work finished on two safety barriers running along the outer edge of the bridge walkways that straddle the road's perimeter. A couple of metres higher than the original railings, they arc over the walkway so they're difficult to scale. Stretched along their length is soft stainless-steel mesh.

In 2014 researchers from Griffith University used data from the Queensland Suicide Registry to show that suicides from the Gateway Bridge, another high Brisbane bridge, were reduced by 87.3 per cent after safety railings were installed in 1993. The Story Bridge safety railings were stuck in bureaucratic channels for years—the idea was first proposed in 2003, and approved in 2010, but it took five years from that point for their construction to begin.

According to a Brisbane City Council briefing note, the reason the railings took so long to erect was partly because of structural considerations and partly because of aesthetic considerations. The bridge is used in marketing images—any visual alterations require serious paperwork.

Patrick told me about this extended inception period for the safety barriers. Almost crying with anger, he said, 'If it hadn't taken so long Alexander would still be here.'

A few years ago I was discussing the premise of this book with a friend, who said, 'The problem with Australia is that it's a nanny state. Why should I have to go home at 1 a.m. because some idiots can't control their fists when they're drinking?' On the one hand, I agree with her. There's magic to cities—like Berlin, Buenos Aires and Paris—that never close. Those places are exciting, buzzing and imbued with a sense of freedom, which doesn't seem to exist so much in Australian cities, especially those that shut down early.

On the other hand, there are many simple designs that might

have made all the difference on the night Alexander died. Maybe if alcohol was more expensive, he couldn't have afforded to drink so much; maybe if the responsible-service-of-alcohol laws were better enforced or better designed, the bar staff could easily have implemented them, and my brother would have been cut off at a certain point; maybe if the people he had been with were more aware of drinking safety (although how many times have I walked home alone, extremely drunk, after refusing assistance); maybe if the bar had closed earlier and he had left before his blood was quite so saturated with ethanol; maybe if the safety barriers along the bridge's railing had been built—maybe my brother would have lived.

In September 2015 an article entitled 'Presentations with alcohol-related serious injury to a major Sydney trauma hospital after 2014 changes to liquor laws' was published in the *Medical Journal of Australia*. It reported that, in the twelve months following the introduction of the city's lockout zone, 'there was a significant reduction in the number of alcohol-related serious injury and trauma presentations to the [nearest] emergency department... This change was seen throughout the week, but was especially marked at weekends.'

Perhaps this is what living in a community where people, and particularly young people, die unnecessarily from drinking is about. While most of us are allowed and encouraged to consume a product that releases our inhibitions, we need also to accept some measures that are put in place for those people who might react badly to that consumption, because they are unhappy, or because their physiology means they are affected by alcohol consumption in such a way that they become violent or suicidal, or because they don't have the means—somewhere regular to sleep, a way of getting home, companions to look out for them—to recover from drunkenness safely.

That doesn't mean excusing the dangerous, harmful actions of drunk individuals, but it does mean accepting that alcohol is not an ordinary commodity, and that trying to contain its effects at the time of consumption is less messy than dealing with them afterwards, even if harm-prevention measures somewhat constrain our access to aesthetic or sensual pleasure. It doesn't negate the need for cultural change—but until that change occurs, and a significant decrease in underage drinking shows that it is, it's better to have measures in place.

I wish that Alexander had had the chance to mess up in small ways over and over again. I wish, aged thirty, he had lain in bed all day vomiting and thinking, I'm too old for this. I wish he had had a chance to hear Dad say, 'at some point, you just have to stop,' and know that it was probably true, even if he was unsure whether he would be able to stop. I wish he had been able to smack his head on the doors of epiphany enough times that they finally opened up and he was changed, or enough times that he fell over, and just accepted that he might not change but at least he was alive.

And, if he did want to die, I wish he had considered it sober, and talked about it with someone, or at least written a letter of explanation. I wish he hadn't had the opportunity, liquored up and full of bravado, or sadness, or whatever he was feeling, to fly off the side of the bridge.

Because, although I always knew in theory that the inexplicable, untimely death of someone I loved unreservedly would be awful, what was impossible to know until it actually happened was that afterwards there would no longer be a time when I was not a little bit sad. And that my sadness would not be noble and acute—it would be dull, empty, endless, selfish, angry and irritating. It would be there when I was at dinner with my family, when I was fucking, when I was alone and when I was not. It would embarrass me while I was walking or eating a sandwich.

It would feel perpetually like being on the edge of a sneeze or an orgasm or a new relationship, and never being able to get there. The satisfaction of feeling whole, of coming to a conclusion, of knowing what was what, would be gone. It seemed I would always be wondering: What happened? Why did it happen? And then: What a waste of a life that was.

ACKNOWLEDGMENTS

Thank you to: Dr Mark Daglish, Dr Anthony Lynham, Paul Stanley, Chris Raine, Patrick McAnelly, Matthew Tetstall, Jon Perring, and Andy Gourley, who were so generous with their time and words.

Alexander's incredible friends: Toddy, Matt, Kieran, AJ, and Jon, for their frank and fearless storytelling.

Xochi, Hamish, Kylie, Craig, Laura, and Annaliese, who let me pilfer our past for anecdotes, and who are hilarious and astonishing.

Sam Cooney, who was the first person to ask me for stories.

Stuart Glover, who, four years ago, agreed to answer one question, and who has been answering my questions ever since.

Stephen Lewin, who helped me get a job when I was running out of money and laughed at me when I was being neurotic; and Alison McGuckin and Alison Campbell, who always accommodated my last-minute requests for time off.

Marde, Yonna, Teresa, and Duncan, who gave me their time, stories, sage advice, and encouragement for many years, and without whom I would have given up many times.

My extended family, friends, and generous strangers: Gran, Tonya, Virginia, Johanna, the Muirs, the Wards, the Sorensons, the Heatleys, the Laws, the Meerdings, the Bryans, the Gores, the Tozers, Clare McEniery, Chanelle Moar, Adriana Velez, TVDC, Cory Taylor, Ashley Hay, and Marie Williams.

The wonderful people at Text, especially Chong Weng Ho, who designed the beautiful cover. David Winter, my editor, who took a chance on me; who was kind, insightful, thoughtful and brilliant; and who exercised inhuman patience over the many unscheduled extra years it took to complete the book.

To my family: Dymphna, Chris, and Patrick Muir, who are so tough. Thanks for letting me write this story.